The Public Library in the United States

THE GENERAL REPORT OF THE PUBLIC LIBRARY INQUIRY

OF THE SOCIAL SCIENCE RESEARCH COUNCIL

THE GENERAL REPORT OF THE PUBLIC LIBRARY
INQUIRY

The
Public Library
in the
United States

By Robert D. Leigh

1950

COLUMBIA UNIVERSITY PRESS · NEW YORK

THE RESEARCH UPON WHICH THIS STUDY IS BASED WAS MADE POSSIBLE BY FUNDS GRANTED BY CARNEGIE CORPORATION OF NEW YORK TO THE SOCIAL SCIENCE RESEARCH COUNCIL FOR THE PUBLIC LIBRARY INQUIRY. THE CARNEGIE CORPORATION IS NOT, HOWEVER, THE AUTHOR, OWNER, PUBLISHER, OR PROPRIETOR OF THIS PUBLICATION, AND IS NOT TO BE UNDERSTOOD AS APPROVING BY VIRTUE OF ITS GRANT ANY OF THE STATEMENTS MADE OR VIEWS EXPRESSED THEREIN.

COMMITTEE FOR THE
PUBLIC LIBRARY INQUIRY

Foreign and International Developments: RICHARD H. HEINDEL, U.S. Senate Committee on Foreign Relations.

Mass Media: JOSEPH T. KLAPPER, Bureau of Applied Social Research.

Music Materials: OTTO LUENING, Professor of Music, Columbia University; assisted by H. R. Shawhan, and Eloise Moore.

Government Publications: JAMES L. McCAMY, Professor of Political Science, University of Wisconsin; assisted by Julia B. McCamy.

Book Publishing: WILLIAM MILLER, writer and historian.

Library Processes: WATSON O'D. PIERCE, formerly Vice President, Nejelski & Company.

Special Projects: HELEN R. ROBERTS, formerly with the Commission on Freedom of the Press.

Films: GLORIA WALDRON, Twentieth Century Fund; assisted by Cecile Starr.

Administrative Assistant: LOIS A. MURKLAND.

FOREWORD

THE PUBLIC LIBRARY in the United States is taken for granted. Predominantly local in character, both in support and management, it is deeply rooted in our national heritage. The community's library stands for much that is cherished in our tradition of equal educational opportunity and freedom of thought and communication. It takes its place along with the courthouse, the school, the church, and the town hall as an integral part of the American scene.

But what do we know about the actual operations and problems of this firmly established institution? An opportunity to add to our existing knowledge was welcomed by the Social Science Research Council when a proposal to examine the American public library was made by the American Library Association and financial support for the study was offered by the Carnegie Corporation of New York.

The Council assumed the responsibility of developing plans for the study, appointing Robert D. Leigh, a political scientist, as its director and associating with him an advisory committee to lend guidance and criticism. The staff to carry on the inquiry brought together specialists from various fields, attracted by the chance to apply their distinctive methods of analysis to a single social institution. The Public Library Inquiry provided this group with an unusual opportunity for research. The individual investigators were free to pursue their own methods of inquiry. They had the full co-operation of the librarians in the gathering of data. The advisory committee reviewed their work at ten meetings over a two-year period, but the reports are the responsibility of the individual authors. Specialists from the various social science disciplines seldom have the opportunity to work as a team on a large-scale, systematic inquiry with direct access through field work to the situation under scrutiny. In this sense the Public Library Inquiry can be regarded as an experiment that may have a value well beyond its contribution to a better understanding of public library problems.

In any such study there are certain limitations. Those conducting the research necessarily did so from the outside. They brought to their task the objective attitude characteristic of the research man who is not identified with the institution under study. At the same time, they lacked that intuitive familiarity with their subject matter that is only the product of direct operating experience. The interview must be relied upon heavily as a means of gathering data, and this method has shortcomings of which social scientists are well aware. The questionnaire is another necessary, though far from perfected, tool. The inquiry started with a careful scrutiny of the rather substantial literature concerning library problems and activities, but has gone well beyond anything attempted in previous studies through the use of various analytical methods. For example, carefully devised opinion polling procedures were used, and existing surveys were analyzed in an effort to ascertain public attitudes toward the library and the uses to which it is now being put.

One of the inescapable difficulties in evaluating the public library as a social institution is the scarcity of comparative information. How little is known in any systematic way of other institutions or professions was emphasized when comparable data were sought by which to appraise libraries and librarians. Indeed, one effect of the problems of the inquiry may be to stimulate further study of professional groups in this country.

Special studies of the inquiry examined the distribution of governmental publications, the use of informational films and music recordings, and the operation of the book industry. Other studies reviewed the control and administration of public libraries, their book resources, technical processes, financial and other problems of organization and personnel. The general report presented in the pages which follow brings these separate studies together. It is a summary account of public library structure and operations set in the perspective of the objectives which librarians have defined and the vision they have held concerning their social responsibilities. Above all, it relates the public library to the groups using it and to significant development in the broad fields of education and mass communication.

The study as a whole is designed to stimulate public librarians to re-examine realistically their most useful function and greatest potential contribution at a time when methods of communication are undergoing rapid change. As the traditional custodian of the printed word, the librarian has long had a distinctive and widely accepted role. The Public Library Inquiry, especially in the concluding chapter of the present volume, brings to the center of attention problems and suggestions for change challenging a fresh appraisal. It should arouse the interest of the public served by the libraries as well as aid the librarians themselves to an appreciation of an important American institution that must be kept ever alert to the needs of a democratic society.

PENDLETON HERRING
PRESIDENT, SOCIAL SCIENCE
RESEARCH COUNCIL

New York City
April 30, 1950

CONTENTS

CONTENTS

The Public Library in
the United States

I

THE PUBLIC LIBRARY INQUIRY

NEARLY THREE YEARS AGO the American Library Association asked the Social Science Research Council to make a study of the public library in the United States. With a grant of $200,000 for the purpose from the Carnegie Corporation, the Council agreed to undertake the inquiry and appointed the author of this volume to direct it. A staff of twenty-four research associates and assistants, some on a part-time basis, was chosen by the director to carry on special studies and a committee of the Council was designated to serve in an advisory capacity. The present volume brings together the findings of the director and staff in a general, final report, addressed to librarians, library boards, other public officials, and citizens generally who are concerned with present public library practice and with library development in the decade ahead.

Although the report rests primarily on the nineteen special studies carried on by the staff and profits greatly from the criticism and guidance of the members of the Advisory Committee for the Inquiry, the interpretations, judgments, and conclusions contained in it are made solely on the author's responsibility.

The request made by the American Library Association to the Social Science Research Council was for "an appraisal in sociological, cultural, and human terms of the extent to which the librarians are achieving their objectives," and "an assessment of the public library's actual and potential contribution to American society." Thus the problem set for the Inquiry was twofold: to appraise public libraries in terms of their own stated objectives and to appraise the appropriateness of the objectives themselves against the background of American social and cultural institutions and values.

SCOPE   The scope of the Inquiry was limited to the public library in the United States broadly interpreted to include all libraries, however supported and controlled, which provide free services intended for the general public. Isolation of the public library for special study presented some difficulties. It is not hard to distinguish the public library in the average community, with its Greek colonnades and portico, from the library on the university campus, in the high school building, or in the industrial research laboratory. But actually their tasks overlap, notably those of public libraries and university and research libraries. The largest city and state libraries, such as the New York, Boston, Cleveland, and California (state) libraries, are both popular and research institutions of the first rank. Furthermore, the country's major research libraries, especially the Library of Congress, serve as a backlog for municipal public libraries, supplying books not on the local library shelves, bibliographies on special subjects, and centrally printed catalogue cards. Also, there are vital relationships between the school library and the children's division of the public library, and between public and special libraries. The latter nearly always use public libraries as a resource for less-used materials. In some communities, as in Chicago, there is an acknowledged division of labor between the tax-supported public library, the endowed research and special libraries, and the university libraries. In the broadest sense all types of libraries here and in other countries form a loose international network performing the common function of storing, arranging, and making available for current and later use the world's recorded events, ideas, and facts of all kinds deemed worthy of preservation.

But the Public Library Inquiry did not have the assignment or the resources to study all libraries. Consequently, they concentrated on the community's tax-supported institution, with the Greek colonnades, but with eyes open to the relationships of these public libraries to all other types of libraries and library services.

TOOLS OF SOCIAL SCIENCE   That the librarians asked the social scientists to undertake a study of libraries has given the Inquiry something of a special character. Surveys of single public libraries, of special aspects of library service, and of libraries as a whole have been frequent in the United States. Almost without exception, however, they have been studies of libraries by librarians. Here was a request for an independent study of libraries by a group whose only connection with libraries was as users.

What advantage was to be expected from an inquiry by a group of outsiders? Certainly it could not be assumed that their ignorance of library practice constituted any qualification for the task. But their very detachment from library affiliation might be an aid to objectivity, especially as social scientists accept objectivity as a primary canon. Thus, an independent group might see some things differently from the most conscientious group of library practitioners, inevitably bound as the librarians must be by the subtle, often unconscious, commitments inherent in their professional responsibilities and positions of leadership. It might also be expected that social scientists had available some tools for inquiry more refined and accurate than personal impressions and individual insights and that in their analysis of other social institutions they had accumulated general ideas about institutional purpose, structure, and process, relevant for an analysis of public libraries.

In the prosecution of its work the Inquiry has made an effort to meet these three expectations. Detachment from official or unofficial library controls has been rigorously maintained. None of the members chosen for the staff was a practicing librarian; all were from the social science disciplines or one of the communications fields. On the advisory committee, along with an economist, an historian, a psychologist, a political scientist, and a sociologist, there were two librarians. But although the librarian members participated fully with the other committee members in the review of the staff and director's reports—indeed at times disagreed with staff findings and conclusions, as did the nonlibrarian members—the author of each of the reports, after review and criticism, was left free to publish facts, judgments, and conclusions as he saw them.

The tools of inquiry used by the staff were, as far as ingenuity could adapt them, those developed in the social science fields. The specific methods employed are described in the appendix to this volume and in the special studies themselves. It would be misleading to claim that they are more than a modest beginning in the application of social science techniques to the study of a single social institution.

Social science as yet has built no comprehensive conceptual framework resting on extended, rigorous research which can be brought to bear on the study of the public library. But the director and staff as students did bring with them to the Inquiry basic conceptions of social goals generally accepted in our culture and some generalizations derived from examination of other social institutions. These were made explicit at the outset of the Inquiry in the form of assumptions or premises.

INQUIRY ASSUMPTIONS   The assumptions were not arrived at in any considerable degree by quantitative method or through controlled experiment. Clearly they are set in the ideological as well as material framework within which the public library and other American social institutions operate: a free, democratic society which is at the same time a society of large geographic extent and one which makes full use of modern science and technology. If we had been living and working within a totalitarian or feudal society, some of our assumptions would have been different. We were not oblivious to the fact that the public library is in no sense a peculiarly democratic instrument. Indeed, our survey of recent public library developments throughout the world indicated that fascist and communist countries have been most active in promoting public library growth within their borders. But their libraries do not operate under assumptions such as have guided library developments in democratic countries.

Our assumptions derive in part, therefore, from values not universally held and whose authority is other than scientific. To some the values are considered to be natural laws, self-evident, hallowed by sacrifice, perhaps revealed through sacred writing or dogma. To us as social scientists they are plausible hypotheses representing man's accumulated insights derived from the long experience of living together. As hypotheses they are subject to continued testing and verification. For the purposes of this single inquiry, however, they served rather as premises underlying the structure and interpretations of our analysis of public library objectives and practice.

The assumptions consist in every case of pairs of values or generalizations which often encounter each other as opposites in institutional theory and practice. The tensions which result must be accepted as the climate within which practical decisions are made.

The six asumptions are defined in the paragraphs which follow.

1) *Opportunity to learn.* The democratic principle of individual opportunity applies especially to opportunity to learn. Consequently, a democratic society will seek to provide generally for its members the means of civic enlightenment, of

occupational and avocational knowledge, and of varied kinds of personal development and satisfactions. Democracy has a special interest in providing the means of civic enlightenment. For enlightenment on public affairs serves not only personal enrichment but is also a necessary basis for the transaction of the business of a democratic state—even for its survival.

On the other hand, opportunity to learn, although offered equally, will not be availed of equally by all people. Differing intellectual capacities and different degrees and kinds of interests and desires are basic realities in any general population. This means that learning will, in fact, be unequal in quality and amount and that the machinery providing opportunity to learn must be adjusted to these individual differences of capacity and desire if it is to avoid waste and ineffectiveness.

2) *Freedom of communication.* Free personal expression and communication are both an individual right, which free governments are designed to protect as a good in itself, and a basic social value. A civilized society keeps its vitality through the general adoption of new ideas, insights, and forms of expression originating with individuals and minorities, which through the process of criticism, develop into prevailing conceptions. A free society, therefore, in its long-term interest, makes available through public communication as many as possible of the ideas and insights which its members express.

Some of the innovating thought, however, is crude, indefensible, even dangerous. It has ranged against it not only the inertia of habit but also the opposition of those wielding social power who feel a responsibility for maintaining standards of decency, order, and morality. In even the freest societies, therefore, there are some prohibitions against communication of material because of its real or reputed harmful effect. Freedom of public communication is never an absolute, but always a relative matter in practice, symbolized in our culture by the semantic device of reserving the term liberty for that which is permitted and license for that which is banned.

3) *Popular control and expert direction.* Public institutions carrying on specialized activities are properly subject to expert direction. Professional management is committed to applying expert knowledge for the benefit of the institution's clientele. This exercise of professional judgment, however, is always a delegated function. In a democracy, professional administration will be checked by the lay opinion of the community and will be subject to its ultimate control. Actual institutional policy, then, represents the interaction, and often will reflect the tensions, between expert and lay judgments. Reduction of the tensions by abdication of the professional function or of the lay check reduces either the dynamics of expert knowledge or the stability resulting from popular controls.

4) *Special groups and the mediating function.* In countries such as the United States, with its great geographical extent and its advanced degree of industrialization and urbanization, the easy interchange of fact, opinion, and attitude across neighborhood and occupational lines, characteristic of our earlier village communities, is replaced in part by groupings along lines of occupation, economic status, nationalism, and religion. These groups are often highly organized internally, but insulated from each other, so that different groups come to live in somewhat separated worlds of fact and judgment and require specialized services of all sorts adjusted to their level of discourse.

For purposes of cohesion and effective political action on a large scale such countries have an especial interest in cultivating those institutions which serve the whole community, avoid identification with limited, partisan segments of the population, and occupy a position as the meeting ground for persons of diverse types and backgrounds, constituting an effective symbol of communal fraternity.

5) *Centralization and local participation.* To carry on a common government over a continental area requires a considerable degree of centralization and large-scale administration and supervision. Furthermore, any real attempt to equalize public services involves centralization of some sort to reduce the inequalities which are bound to exist in a country which is characterized by uneven distribution of population and economic resources and where the public services are supported by independent, local units.

On the other hand, a democracy depends for its continued vitality on encouraging widespread local initiative and citizen participation, by multiplying the points of direct contact between the citizen and the public official and by adapting public services as far as possible to the variant interests and conditions of different communities. In the organization of public services in a democracy which is also a great society, therefore, these two often-conflicting objectives need to be reconciled rather than to sacrifice one completely to the other.

6) *Technological change and institutional tradition.* Social institutions with long continuity of essential structure and with professionally organized personnel are sensitive to the values of tradition and tend to stress awareness of the past. They serve as conservators of the classical and permanently valuable in knowledge, morals, and taste.

Contemporary culture is characterized, however, by a wealth of invention and experiment which impose steady pressures on institutions for alterations in their structure and habits. The changes are often far-reaching, at times even involving the shift of functions from one institution to another. This is especially true of the impact of technological inventions, which seem to possess a highly volatile character compared with nonmaterial elements in the culture.

It can be expected, then, that technological and other changes will press upon nearly every institution in our society and that they will be resisted. In this situation, economy of social action dictates awareness by institutional leaders of those practices which are justified merely as institutional habits and to the necessity of adapting their practices to promising innovations. At the same time, economy of social action dictates that institutional leaders shall not reverse their favorable judgment of existing practice because of innovation which promises little else than novelty.

Our examination of the objectives, function, structure, organization, services, and personnel of public libraries in the chapters which follow is set in the background of these six assumptions—assumptions which apply to institutions in a democratic, continental, industrial, and urban society. We should expect to find that in some form or degree the conflicting concepts and values will appear in the description of library policy and practice. In the public library's attempt to reconcile them we would expect to locate some of its major problems.

2

THE LIBRARY FAITH AND
LIBRARY OBJECTIVES

LIBRARIES OF ALL KINDS during the centuries of their existence have had a common objective—one so generally accepted that it is seldom made explicit. It is the conservation and organization of the world's resources of recorded thought and fact so as to make them available for present and future users. This is an obvious utility for any civilization as soon as it feels the need for something more than oral tradition. And the library, including the public library, has become in most places a kind of symbol as well as servant of culture.

THE LIBRARY FAITH   Throughout the years librarians have transformed their concept of function into a dynamic faith. This faith has sustained the men and women who have built and operated American public, as well as university and research, libraries and the men of wealth and political position who have provided for their financial and legal support. It consists of a belief in the virtue of the printed word, especially of the book, the reading of which is held to be good in itself or from its reading flows that which is good.

Our review of American library development[1] indicates that

[1]Oliver Garceau, *The Public Library in the Political Process; a Report of the Public Library Inquiry,* New York, Columbia University Press, 1949. See especially, Chapter 1, "The Foundations of Library Government." Throughout the present volume, material and phraseology will be reproduced or summarized from the Inquiry staff reports, and hereafter specific footnote references to them will not be made. In the Appendix of the present volume there is a description of the sources of the material, chapter by chapter.

at different periods the specific virtues to be promoted by the
reading of books and, therefore, by libraries, have varied in
rough correspondence with the general outlook or *Zeitgeist*.
In colonial times the Protestant revolt which elevated private
conscience to a decisive role made individual reading of the
Book, if not of books, a necessary religious act. Later, when
self-governing commonwealths and a central government were
being created out of the colonies, there was emphasis on reading as a means of providing the citizenry with the learning
necessary for a sound collective judgment on public affairs.
As the nation expanded westward and economic opportunities
were broadened in exploitation of the resources of a continent,
the free storehouse of books was seen as providing opportunity for persons of ability, "otherwise doomed to obscurity by
poverty," to gain knowledge useful for their personal advancement. As urban life and leisure developed and the "dissipations
of the tavern and brothel" seemed to multiply, the reading of
books and building of libraries were often promoted by the
town fathers as a means of providing "more rational and profit-
able" forms of amusement. When radicalism reared its head in
labor and agrarian circles, there were those who argued for
libraries as agencies to enhance stability and conservatism by
reading about the economic facts of life. When people from
Southern and Eastern Europe, having strange customs and
dialects, seemed to be inundating our cities, the public library,
with its store of books, was hopefully turned to as a means of
assimilating the recent immigrants into our cultural pattern.

The object here is not to assess the practicality or effectiveness of these successive, overlapping beliefs in the ameliorative
function of books and libraries, but to establish the fact that
virtue in books has been the traditional faith of the American
librarian. Interpreted modestly, in terms of the obvious value
of providing ready materials for seekers after knowledge to
serve a variety of individual purposes, the public librarian has

seen his faith justified daily in good works. In its more ambitious form as a belief in the power of books to transform common attitudes, to combat evils, or to raise the cultural level, the public librarian's faith has in it an element of magic in words as substitutes for realities. Recently, because of the heterogeneous output of current print and pictures within board or paper covers, the virtue claimed for books has had to be qualified. At least it becomes a magic of Great Books. But in one way or another the tradition that books possess a precious ameliorative quality continues to provide the public librarian with a sense of significance in his daily work.

THE CURRENT OBJECTIVES   Fortunately, we are not limited to deducing current public library objectives from library history and observed practice. Three statements of objectives for public libraries in the United States, bearing the stamp of approval of the American Library Association, have been promulgated in the last six years. The first appeared in 1943 as Chapter 2 of the booklet entitled *Post-War Standards for Public Libraries*, prepared by the Committee on Post-War Planning of the ALA. This committee, consisting of five leading members of the library profession, was aided by a group of twenty-six consultants, half of whom were public library officials, eight were members of library school faculties, and the others holders of posts in the ALA or other library organizations. The consultants met, revised, and approved the draft of the booklet. The second statement appeared as part of the first chapter of *A National Plan for Public Library Service*, issued in 1948, also by the ALA Committee on Post-War Planning. The draft of the *National Plan* was approved by a smaller group of eight consultants, preliminary drafts were "sent to many librarians for criticism and suggested revision," and were finally approved by the Association's governing body, the ALA Council. The third statement, entitled

Four Year Goals, prepared by officers of the ALA, was also officially approved by its Council early in 1948. Inasfar as wide participation in criticism and responsible sponsorship can make them, these statements may be considered official public library objectives, reflecting a consensus of the judgments of American public library leadership.

In order that we might assure ourselves that the statements of objectives represent public library thinking outside official circles also, the Public Library Inquiry combined the three documents into one, eliminating only obvious duplications of phraseology. The consolidated statement was mailed to the librarians in the Inquiry sample, consisting of sixty public libraries of all sizes, located in various regions of the country.[2] Copies were sent also to nineteen state librarians, to eleven city librarians in larger communities outside the sample, to eleven library school faculty members, and to ten university librarians and other library officials known to be interested in public library problems. Thus, altogether the consolidated statement was given to 110 persons, only ten of whom were members of the ALA Committee on Post-War Planning. With the statement went the request to indicate "to what extent it is accurate and adequate in defining the working objectives toward which public libraries really direct their plans and efforts." The librarians were asked to give their "own revisions or independent statements at any places considered not realistic or right."

Replies were received from 80 percent of the whole group, including 82 percent of the librarians in the Inquiry sample. Five sixths of those who replied accepted the statement of objectives as sound and accurate, and many said that as librarians they did their best to achieve them. A number of librarians from smaller libraries added that they could not carry out the

[2]See Appendix, pp. 252-255, for list of the libraries in the Inquiry sample and for an explanation of how they were chosen.

objectives to any extent because of inadequate funds and personnel.

Clearly, although opinion was not unanimous, there was a consensus in approval of the objectives. Only two librarians rejected the whole statement as inaccurate or misleading. Concerning four points in the document, however, a minority, each very small numerically, dissented with considerable conviction. These minority dissents will be described below. Making full allowance for them, however, the document may be accepted as setting forth the aims of most public librarians in the United States.

The consolidated statement consists of three parts: *A)* a general definition of public library objectives; *B)* a more extended definition of the fields of knowledge and interest to which library activities should be directed; *C)* a definition of public library activities suitable for attaining the objectives. If one considers public libraries as educational institutions, only the first of the three parts might be called the objectives; the other two parts define the curriculum and the method of achieving the objectives.

The statement follows.[3]

A) General Definition of Objectives

1) To assemble, preserve, and administer books and related educational materials in organized collections, in order to promote, through guidance and stimulation, an enlightened citizenship and enriched personal lives.

2) To serve the community as a general center of reliable information.

[3]The statement reproduced here differs from that sent to the 110 librarians only by the addition of minor textual improvements suggested by the librarians themselves and the elimination of four phrases to which there were a number of objections: i.e., "vocational guidance," as a library function; the phrase, "people's university"; special mention of aesthetic appreciation of twentieth-century culture; the library's "making it difficult for anyone to remain ignorant or apathetic about the great public issues of our time." These changes do not alter the substance of the statement.

3) To provide opportunity and encouragement for children, young people, men, and women to educate themselves continuously.

B) *Fields of Knowledge and Interest to Which the Public Library Should Devote Its Resources*

1) *Public affairs; citizenship*

   a) To awaken interest, stimulate reading and discussion on crucial problems;

   b) To improve people's ability to participate usefully in activities in which they are involved as citizens of their communities, the United States, and the world;

   c) To help people develop a constructively critical attitude toward all public issues and to remove ignorance regarding them;

   d) To promote democratic attitudes and values; i.e., sensitivity toward peoples of other backgrounds by knowledge concerning them and by appreciation of the dignity of the individual person; preservation of the precious heritage of freedom of expression; and understanding of the democratic processes of group life.

2) *Vocations*

   To equip persons, and to keep them equipped, for efficient activities in useful occupations and practical affairs (including vocational information, parent and home education, child care, nutrition, physical health, emotional stability and growth, budgeting and consumer information, specialized business and industrial information).

3) *Aesthetic appreciation*

   To seek to give people an opportunity to improve their capacity for appreciation and production in cultural fields.

4) *Recreation*

   To help people make such use of leisure time as will promote personal happiness and social well-being.

5) *Information*

   To help people keep abreast of progress in the sciences

and other fields of knowledge, and to furnish them with
the detailed information required for their personal projects and everyday needs.

6) *Research*

To serve those who are aiding in the advancement of
knowledge.

C) *Library Means for Attaining the Library Objectives*

1) *Kinds of materials*

Library collections are founded on the printed page, but
should be supplemented by films, recordings, and radio;
also by lectures, forums, and discussion groups.

2) *Availability of materials*

By selection and organization libraries should make an educational instrument out of a welter of records; by co-
operative acquisition, inter-library loans, and book pools
they should insure to their patrons accessibility to the
world's useful knowledge; their materials should be free
to all residents on equal terms; and library service should
be established where it is not now available.

3) *Guidance*

Librarians should mediate between seekers for knowledge
and the recorded materials which contain and increase
knowledge, thus eliminating the gap between the seekers
and sources of information and ideas.

4) *Stimulation and leadership*

Libraries should have a positive program of stimulation in
the use of library materials, selecting subjects for emphasis
with the view to replacing indifference by interest, and of
exercising an influence on what people think about, without attempting to tell them what conclusions they should
reach.

The library, in co-operation with all other agencies of
education and information, should seek to increase the
competence of people to form sound judgments and to realize that they should not only understand about important public problems, but also express their opinions and
act in accordance with their judgment.

The library should assist in the establishment and improvement of community group programs, and adapt programs to the interests of special groups. At the same time, the library's duty remains that of providing reliable information on all sides of controversial questions.

5) *Emphasis*

During the next four years (1948–52), librarians should change the intensity, the duration, and even the nature of their services so that they will contribute directly to the solution of the crucial problems of our time.

They should make sure that opinion leaders and other citizens have the widest possible range of reliable information on which to base their judgments and action.

Libraries should provide themselves with generous supplies of these materials even if by so doing it means some curtailment of acquisition of popular and general materials.

Setting this current statement of public library objectives alongside the librarian's historic faith reveals a strong family resemblance between the two. The individual and social values which derive from a reading of books is central to both. But in the newer statement of objectives there are significant extensions of the traditional definition of purpose. The public library's function is explicitly broadened to include other materials of communication, including non-print materials. Perhaps more important, the faith in the mere presence of a community book collection as a power to change people's ideas, attitudes, and tastes is now transformed into a positive program for libraries to guide, stimulate, and promote public use of public library materials for educational ends.

Indeed, certain phrases in the original text of the official objectives containing strong imperatives to librarians to change peoples' motives, habits, and ideas seem to assume that the great desirability of such changes somehow establishes the practical possibility of effecting them. For example, the following passage urges public librarians to "help measurably to abolish indifference . . . exercising an influence on what people think about . . . increase the competence of people to form sound judgments . . . make it difficult for anyone within its span of influence to remain ignorant or apathetic about the great public issues of our time." This tendency to brush aside stubborn realities concerning the possibility of accomplishment by stressing the reality of need has in it the same word magic which was noted as occasionally present in the earlier affirmations of the librarian's faith. Allowing for their exaggerated assumption of the possibilities of attainment, however, the current official objectives have a consistent logic as a program of general out-of-school education.

DISSENTS FROM CURRENT OBJECTIVES   Most of the minority dissents from the official objectives are based on a concern lest they include too much territory within the public library domain. Four librarians raised some question about, and two others objected strongly (the six constituting only 7 percent of all responding) to, the inclusion of materials other than books as legitimate library resources, especially to such activities as lectures, forums, and discussion groups. Two of the six felt that the general public library objective was completely stated in the phrase "to make books useful to people." At the other extreme were two library leaders who felt that there should be no preference for print, but that public libraries should assemble materials of all kinds impartially. Quite evidently these are the two end points on the broad spectrum of library opinion so far as it is revealed in the sample. The official statement, which keeps books in a preferred place, but admits other materials as auxiliaries, seems to have the general support of the members of the profession.

The second kind of dissent is not so much dissent as misgiving on the part of a small minority regarding the extent to which the public library should move away from the limited function of stimulation and guidance in the use of library materials to become a general agency of out-of-school education. Eight librarians raised questions in one form or another regarding this matter.[4] One asked: "Are librarians teachers, or are they rather the keepers and organizers of the instruments of education and stimulators of their use?"

On the other side, three librarians would go further than the official objectives; they would set up the public library as the chief institution of adult education and conduct classes, reading clinics, and so forth, administering materials as only one of the instruments in a general educational program.

In fact, the official objectives can be interpreted to justify this assumption of an unlimited educational function. Our reading of them, however, leads to the conclusion that they retain the skilled provision of materials, including services related to materials, as the center of public library activity. Judged by the returns from the sample, the large majority of librarians approve of this active but specialized role of the public library in out-of-school enlightenment.

The third point of dissent is also a question as to emphasis rather than any logical disagreement. Eight librarians "could not go along" with the section in the document calling for a stress upon public affairs in public libraries during the next four years. All of the eight considered public affairs a proper part of a balanced library program. They were opposed only to destroying balance in their library collections and in library services. As was true of dissent on the other matters, however, the dissenters were matched by four librarians who stated that in usual library practice public affairs were slighted in comparison with most of the other areas of knowledge and inter-

[4]The dissenters enumerated in these paragraphs are in many cases not different persons but the same persons objecting to more than one aspect of the objectives. Only 16 percent of the group replying expressed dissent or misgiving regarding any substantive part of the combined statement.

est. Such comment, together with the general approval of this part of the objectives, may indicate that the proposal to place a special, immediate emphasis on public affairs is, in fact, moving toward a better balance in public library resources and in services rather than away from it.

The three points of minority dissent discussed above relate to extending public library activity in new directions, not to the basic philosophy of the official objectives. The fourth, however, represents views really opposed to the majority agreement as to what public library objectives should be. This dissent is centered on the place of recreation in public library discussion. Recreation has been for years a ticklish term in library discussions. In many statements it is qualified by the adjective "wholesome" or, as here, by the phrase "such use of leisure time as will promote personal happiness and social well being." The dissenters point out that recreation comprises a large part of present-day public library service to its patrons.

The dissenters really challenge the whole tendency of the document to limit library materials to those dealing with serious and significant personal and social interests. As opposed to this limitation, they say that the public library's function is to give the people what they want whatever the nature and quality of the demand may be. As one phrased it, "Our objective here is the same as the Park Department," providing play for all kinds and ages of people. Another comments: "The public libraries were established in the first place for the people who couldn't afford to buy books . . . we take people as we find them . . . we supply mystery stories in large quantity . . . material for relaxation, entertainment, adventure, escape."

Our letter to the librarians contained the direct query: "Do the current official objectives definitely reject the idea that the library should, within budgetary limits, supply whatever the public demands or asks for?" Twenty-four thought that they clearly implied such rejection; twenty-seven agreed that they did, but that in practice compromises are necessary. But twelve, the largest number of dissenters on any point, felt that the objectives are wrong and impractical if they do not include provision of what the public wants. Here, then, is a minority which freely admits that many books and much reading are without virtue, but that nevertheless the public librarian's task is to supply the books, good or bad, for all comers. They define a viable library service, but renounce the librarian's faith in the ameliorative function of books. The official objectives, and the large majority of librarians in the sample, however, clearly reaffirm that historic faith. In the official objectives there is no mention of the terms "entertainment," "amusement," and "escape." Recreation is given a strict meaning—what is re-creative—but it obviously includes current fiction which falls within this meaning of the term as well as publications which serve the purposes of enlightenment.

Finally, there was an uneasy feeling, expressed by a half dozen librarians, that the official statements are paper pronouncements rather than actual objectives and that they do not really determine practice. One wrote that library objectives were like political party platforms; one has to have them, but once adopted they are ignored by librarians in their day-by-day business. And as has been noted earlier, several small-town librarians said that they have no opposition to the objectives, but that it takes money and personnel, which they do not have, to achieve them. On somewhat the same note, four library-school faculty members felt that objectives general enough to apply to libraries of all sizes are too vague to have meaning for the making of practical library policy in any one of them.

According to our observation of other social institutions in the United States, equal candor on the part of their membership would reveal a similar dichotomy between manifestoes adopted in convention assembled and the specific goals actually aimed at on the job. Adopting objectives and goals evidently serves some ritualistic purpose in our society.

OBJECTIVES AND PERFORMANCE   But objectives cannot be dismissed as so much moonshine. The test of their reality is not whether they are attained completely or in large degree. It is rather whether the announced objectives can and do serve as the actual guide lines when public libraries formulate their programs. Degree of attainment of objectives is important. If a low level of achievement is due primarily to inadequate library organization, structure, personnel, or resources, the defects may be remediable and the objectives may retain their validity. But if the library's traditional purposes have been perpetuated into a current situation in which they no longer have a vital relationship to social needs and to other existing means of providing the same services, lack of adequate public support and organization may reflect the loss of reality of the objectives themselves. In this case the divorce between goals and possible day-to-day achievement may be so complete and so chronic that the objectives become meaningless phrases. Before accepting existing library goals, therefore, as a fixed framework within which to examine current public library organization and operations, we need to appraise the appropriateness of the official objectives against the background of contemporary social and cultural institutions. This means an analysis of the public library as part of the whole business of public communication in the United States.

3

THE BUSINESS OF
COMMUNICATION

FROM THEIR OFFICIAL STATEMENTS OF PURPOSE, it is evident that public librarians conceive of themselves as performing an educational task. The library, however, may also be thought of as a constituent part of public (or mass) communication: the machinery by which words, sounds, and images flow from points of origin through an impersonal medium to hosts of unseen readers and audiences. Communication, in this sense, is even more pervasive than is education. We can hardly conceive of the transaction of the public business or the manifold private activities of a society such as ours, extending over a continental area and having complex commercial, political, and cultural relations with people around the globe, without the services of newspapers, magazines, books, pamphlets and documents, recordings, radio, motion pictures, and television. Together they perform a basic social function. And the public library, collecting and distributing books, magazines, print, and other materials, performs part of that function.

Not only does the library share the total task of communication with other agencies; its operations are also organically related to them. Commercial agencies produce and distribute most of the books and periodicals which the library assembles. And the public library's services to its patrons are in direct, though often unacknowledged, competition with the commercial media. One clue, then, to the discovery of the public library's most appropriate role in contemporary society is to see it against the background of the whole enterprise of public communication.

It is characteristic of the public library as an agency of communication that it is a governmental or noncommercial enterprise whereas most communication agencies are operated as private businesses. The library shares this distinction with the publication and other communication activities of government, universities and colleges, and a few other public or endowed institutions and foundations. But altogether, noncommercial agencies are a relatively small part of the whole machinery of public communication in the United States. Mass communication is largely a profit-seeking business as well as a public service.

THE COMMUNICATIONS REVOLUTION   Newspaper, magazine, and book publication in the United States has always been essentially a private undertaking. Comparatively new, however, is the emergence of very large communication units fashioning their products ingeniously to gain and to hold huge mass markets. This development is so recent, so rapid, and so fundamental that it may properly be called a twentieth-century communications revolution. True, it began more than a century ago with the invention of power-driven printing machinery, and has been followed at intervals by improvements in the printing and engraving processes and in rapid transport and communication of messages, which together ushered in the modern metropolitan daily newspaper. But the appearance of mass magazines (with circulations in the millions), book clubs and chain-store book distribution, the phonograph, the radio, and motion pictures is within the memory of persons now in late middle age.

And the more recent advent of television, of photography as a means of reproducing text cheaply and rapidly on paper or film, and of the electronic transmission of texts page-by-page over great distances, reminds us that we are still in the midst of the communications revolution. It may not be exaggerating to say, as some informed people have said, that the transmission of sights, sounds, and words by electrical impulse will prove as powerful and radical an influence on our political and cultural life as was the invention of printing in the sixteenth century.

Changes such as these, occurring gradually, but adding up over a short period to a major transformation, are usually not accompanied immediately by the necessary adaptations of related social habits and institutional machinery. It would be surprising if the public library had made such an adaptation. For the library appeared and assumed its present institutional form in a world of scarce and expensive books, of equally expensive magazines written for a limited clientele, of newspapers with comparatively narrow range of topics and coverage—a world in which there was no radio, phonograph records, or film. That world differs strikingly from that in which we live today, with its almost bewildering abundance and cheapness of print of all kinds, with news, discussions, pictures, music, and drama, even the facsimile of events themselves as they happen, delivered through film or electric impulse in a constant stream to the citizen-consumer in his office, his home, or other place of relaxation.

THE AUDIENCES OF THE MASS MEDIA   Indeed, the two most striking characteristics of modern mass communication are its sheer abundance and its easy accessibility—one might also say, its obtrusiveness. A public library has thousands of books on its shelves. But a person who wants one of them must go to the library for it. If it is available on the occasion when he calls for it, it is lent to him to read for a limited period. Usually he may not telephone in advance to see whether the trip to the library will be worth while. Almost never, unless he is blind, ill, or otherwise disabled, may he order the book delivered to his home as he habitually does when purchasing groceries or a new hat.

The daily newspaper and the magazine, on the other hand, are delivered to his door; radio and television are his to enjoy in his home by simply turning a knob. In some public places he cannot escape them; he is part of a captive audience. Even the books which he buys may come to him with his morning's mail; those of a limited type which are issued in paper covers or of pocket size may be seen and bought in at least 75,000 stores and newsstands. To see a movie he must bestir himself to go a few blocks to the neighborhood or downtown theater. But there are more than eighteen thousand of these theaters, most of them in convenient locations and open throughout the afternoon and evening seven days a week. There are only about half as many public library buildings in the United States. And the smaller ones (constituting a majority of the whole number) are open only for a limited number of hours daily or weekly.

The citizen response to abundance and accessibility of communication is impressive. It is estimated that the average adult in the United States is engaged for a quarter of his waking hours in reading newspapers, magazines, books, listening to the radio, or seeing movies. If this time were to be consolidated into a continuous period it would occupy all the evening from the end of the family dinner until bedtime. It is half the time devoted daily to sleep; more than the time occupied in eating.

The extent of popular addiction to consuming mass communication, however, differs from one medium to another. Our survey of citizen use and our analysis of other surveys indicate that:

1) Practically all adults listen to the radio and read the newspaper (90 to 95 percent listen to the radio fifteen minutes

or more per day; 85 to 90 percent read one or more news-papers more or less regularly).

2) About two thirds of the adults read some magazine (60 to 70 percent read one or more magazines more or less regularly).

3) About one half of the adults attend the movies periodically (45 to 50 percent see a motion picture once every two weeks or more often).

4) About one fourth of our adult population read books as a habit (25 to 30 percent read one or more books a month, 50 percent claim to have read at least one book in the last year).

In gross numbers of words, pictures, and sounds received per minute by the average adult in the United States, then, books play a relatively minor role. Some of the reasons for this position of book reading are obvious. Both motion pictures and radio reach beyond the group of people able to read; radio is easily available, also, for those who cannot see. The cost of books per unit is greater than for the other media, except for drug-store editions of paper-bound reprints and mysteries. Even with book clubs and free libraries, systems of book distribution are neither so convenient nor so widespread as those of the other media.

As for television, the newest medium to compete for the leisure time of the American people, there are not yet enough sets in use, nor have the purchasers had the sets long enough, to make comparative figures of any great value. From surveys of the present owners of television receivers, however, we find that adults sit before their television screen on an average of two to three hours a day, children almost as many hours daily. These figures, showing extremely heavy use, must be thought of in terms of the present scarcity. We cannot tell what the quantity and extent of use will be when television sets are no longer a novelty, when they have reached a public far wider than the present group of enthusiasts and have become a regular item of home equipment (an audience of fifty million, with nineteen million family sets is the estimate for 1953).

Heretofore each new mass medium, despite predictions to the contrary, has supplemented rather than replaced existing media. Television gives some indication that it may not follow this course. Surveys of television users report a decline of 30 percent in reading during the first six months of ownership, 15 percent a year or more later. They report similarly a drop in movie attendance of 33 percent in the early period, leveling off gradually to approximately 15 percent. The decline in radio listening is greatest. Of the television set owners, 75 to 90 percent say that they listen less to radio, especially during the evening hours when radio has its largest audiences. All these survey figures must be thought of as exploratory and suggestive, rather than definitive. They do indicate, however, that television is likely to take its place as a formidable agency of mass communication with regard to both amount of use and number of users.

When we pass beyond the statistics of average minutes per day of exposure to the various media, some qualifications need to be made. A single radio program of great popularity may have an audience estimated to be thirty million; this number equals the total sales of the fifteen best selling novels for the last five years. Newspaper sales in the United States for five days in 1948 surpassed the total sales of general fiction and nonfiction (trade books) for that year. But these comparisons do not reflect accurately the total exposure to the medium. The day's newspaper goes out with the ash can. A radio program, once heard, is gone with the wind; but the novel *Gone with the Wind* belies its title. It is saved after reading to be lent and read by others; public library copies are used by many readers; it is translated into foreign languages and into the international language of the motion picture. An even longer history of repeated use awaits a book such as Tolstoy's *War and Peace* that becomes a classic in other than the current sense.

Despite these qualifications, however, books remain the most limited of the major agencies of communication so far as numbers in their audiences can be counted. This fact is important to public libraries, because books are the library's principal stock in trade.

THE LIBRARY'S PUBLIC   Public libraries are not the chief distributors of the books that are read by the American people. Defining adults as persons of high school age and beyond, our analyses indicate that about two thirds of the books people read are distributed through commercial channels: 35 to 40 percent by direct purchase; 18 to 25 percent as loans from friends or neighbors, who presumably purchased them or received them as gifts; 7 to 9 percent from commercial rental libraries. Only about one fourth of the books read are from public libraries.[1]

The best estimates from existing data, using the borrowing of one volume or more a month as a basis, are that the public library's clientele for book circulation consists of about 10 percent of the adult population; about 18 percent, if we use the reading of one book a year as the basis. These percentages are considerably less than the proportion of all adults in the average community who by signing a registration card indicate that they intend to borrow books from the public library. It may be more than coincidence that the surveys show the ratio of these library registrants to all adults—usually about one out of four—to be the same as the ratio of adult book readers to all adults in the community. Thus, we may assume that nearly all the community's regular book readers take

[1]In the case of magazine reading, the public library plays a much smaller role than it plays in the reading of books. Only about 2 to 3 per cent of the current periodicals read by adults are the property of public libraries.

out registration cards at one time or another, constituting the public library's potential users, but that only a minority of them at any one time use the library regularly.

If we look at the 10 percent of adults who are regular users of the public library, we are obliged to make one further qualification. The members of this group do not use the library with equal regularity. Here public libraries and book reading are in contrast with some of the other communication media. Nearly all newspaper readers, the studies show, devote about the same amount of time to newspaper reading. Also, the use of radio and magazines is comparatively uniform, though less so than for newspapers. Movie attendance is evidently concentrated as compared with newspapers, radio, or magazines. But concentration is greatest with regard to the use of books, including the borrowing of books from public libraries. The available studies reveal that about 10 percent of the book readers account for about half of all the book reading in the community; and about 10 percent of the public library's borrowers take out one third of all the books borrowed in a two-week period, only 5 percent of the borrowers accounting for two fifths of the annual circulation, 20 percent for three quarters of the books charged out during the year. Clearly, a minority of the 10 percent of adult library users are real library "fans," constituting a larger percentage of the total users of the library than movie and radio fans represent in their total audiences.

So far we have limited ourselves to the use of books, libraries, and the other agencies of communication by adults. The number of children and young people in school who use the libraries is larger in proportion to their total numbers in the population than the proportion of adult library users to the total number of adults. The best estimates indicate that about one third of the former use the library, compared with one tenth of the adults (use being defined as the borrowing of a book once a month or more often). In most communities library registration of juveniles is also proportionately higher than adult registration, usually averaging nearly 50 percent of the juveniles in the population compared with the average 25 percent registration of adults. These figures for juveniles are not based on as reliable or as comprehensive studies as those made of adult library use. And as yet there are no reliable estimates stemming from adequate surveys, of the comparative use by children of books, magazines, radio, newspapers, and movies.

From all the existing data it seems clear that in terms of the total population a small minority of adults and a larger proportion of children, but still a minority, are regular users of public libraries. In no sense does this mean that the library patrons are an inconsequential minority or that public library service is an unimportant segment of the whole machinery of public communication. It means only that in quantitative terms the commercial media reach many more people, even with books.

CELEBRITIES AND PERSONALIZING   The wide coverage of the population attained by the commercial media is not due merely to their abundance and accessibility. It is also the result of careful fashioning of their content and zealous promotion so as to reach the maximum number of consumers. Most mass communication agencies have adopted the usual—probably necessary—techniques of those who make and sell articles for mass markets: standardizing their products, giving them attractive labels, and promoting their sale by extensive and expensive programs of commercial advertising. Indeed, some of the media—radio, newspapers, and magazines—are themselves the instruments for the direct advertising of mass-distributed products as well as for the distribution of ideas, news, and entertainment.

One characteristic of processing for the mass market may be called celebrity-building, or personalizing. We are daily witnesses to this practice in the mass magazines, newspapers, radio, motion pictures, and books, by which attention is centered on stars as authors, actors, or performers rather than upon the content of the subjects dealt with. In some cases the star is created out of obscurity by a careful process of commercial promotion. In other cases a personage well known for activities outside the communication field is used as a ready-made celebrity. A star, once built up by the success of a novel, story, or motion picture, is carefully guided along the path of continued success by variations on the first performance all in the same key. The process of discovering and cultivating celebrities differs somewhat in the various media. But increasingly star-building has become a combined enterprise ranging across the commercial agencies of mass communication. Books are written for and from movies; they are digested in mass magazines; they are distributed by book clubs; authors are guests on radio programs and appear at book fairs, autograph parties, and literary teas fully reported in the newspapers. Star-building is highly competitive; it involves large financial risks. There are frequent flops. Its successes are numerically small, but widely publicized.

The trade-book publishing field, which is of special interest to public libraries, uses this expedient widely. It is apparent in the publisher's choice of volumes promising big sales on which to put his money for promotion. For personalization has a wide appeal. It is a common denominator of interest, reaching out to the marginal, least-interested person, who is the special concern of the medium seeking to saturate the market. The best sellers are of various grades and quality as judged by experts and critics in the fields that the books cover. They usually include each year several publications that eventually join the more permanent contributions to knowledge and literature;

they include some that serve a useful current purpose, but have no permanent use; they include a goodly number of what experts judge to be trash. The important point is that the selection of books for zealous promotion to achieve big sales is made not on the basis of their quality but because of their salability—often a different consideration. In the trade-book publishing field only 150 to 200 of the 4,000 books published each year actually hit the jackpot. But because of best-seller emphasis, the books selected for the big markets are those that most people in any year hear about and read.

The concentration on celebrities and best sellers in book and mass magazine publication is important for public libraries, because it affects directly the current demand for their books. Salability is not an acknowledged basis for the selection of books by an institution performing an educational function. As an educational institution the library might justifiably aim to choose each year from the 4,000 titles those volumes judged by experts to be most reliable and informed in their facts and judgments or of real literary merit rather than those designed to be most salable. It might, then, through lists in newspapers, by the use of an available, donated radio hour, and by book-jacket displays, attempt to bring its annual purchases to the attention of the reading public, and thus have the library's selections more widely read. As compared with the booming, insistent voices of commercial advertisers on behalf of the best sellers, however, the library's promotion is likely to seem a scarcely-audible whisper. In Chapter 5 we shall see that in this situation present library selection of current books is determined for them to a considerable extent by promotion at the hands of commercial media.

SENSATIONALISM AND DISTORTION   Personalization is only one of the devices used by the commercial media which results from the necessity of fashioning the product to the mass market. Equally common as a means of attracting a maximum of readers and audiences are the dramatization of events by sensationalizing them (especially setting them in the formula of combat between personal adversaries), emphasis on the unusual or the forbidden, such as murder, scandal, and sex, or on the dream worlds of mystery and romance. These emphases in selection of the content for communication in the commercial mass media are made in various ways and to different degrees. But they are elementary rules of choice in newspaper and magazine offices, motion picture and radio studios.

A positive result of fashioning the picture of men and events especially so as to reach multitudes is that significant glimpses of the larger world reach many more people than would be the case without such devices. The negative side of the process is that it tends to distort the picture of reality. Life as it is actually lived has much quiet co-operation as well as combat, much drab but useful activity; there are many significant things as well as people; there are complex and related factors which need to be understood in dealing with life's problems. Murder and other crimes are unusual, not normal happenings, as the dull but useful census figures reveal. Communication of the story of men and events in terms of balance and of complex reality may be quite impossible as a function of the media designed to serve audiences of millions. But without such communication smaller but important audiences often numbered in the thousands are left without material they want and need.

AVOIDANCE OF THE UNPOPULAR AND THE EXPERIMENTAL   A third emphasis in the selection of content by the mass media, resulting from the necessity of reaching and holding the largest possible audiences, is the avoidance of ideas that are unpopular or disturbing to a sizable segment of their clientele. The material selected, consequently, tends to reinforce majority ideas, attitudes, and preferences. In a society as heterogeneous as ours this practice probably serves an important positive role. By dramatizing the tradition and emphasizing the major understandings and concepts which have given our society its special character, the media promote unity and stability. The advantage of this emphasis is seen especially in time of war, when such qualities are most needed. On the other hand, we have indicated that we share the democratic assumption that minority views, including disturbing criticisms, have an important function in a free society. And by their selection of content the mass media tend to underemphasize these sometimes unpalatable but germinal ideas and opinions.

In the field of music and the arts there is a somewhat similar tendency on the part of the agencies of large-scale communication to overemphasize the accepted, to repopularize the popular, to underemphasize or to neglect the less celebrated, the new, the unorthodox, and the experimental. The makers and performers of serious music recordings, the music publishers, and the radio broadcasters, for example, present repeatedly what have been called the "Hundred Best Pieces" (the more famous compositions of Beethoven, Brahms, Mozart, Tschaikowsky, Sibelius, Wagner, and a few others). They seldom present the less-well-known works of these same classicists, the preclassical works on which the classics were built, or serious contemporary compositions not yet tested by many performances.

Again, the emphasis of the mass media has important positive aspects. Through the comparatively new machinery of extensive communication many millions of people have for the first time ready access to music of the highest quality performed with the greatest skill. Negatively, however, the commercial media do not extend their programs over the whole range of serious music, but rather, exploit to the full a limited number of compositions which are already famous. In the field of the arts, as in the field of social comment, a balance between the popular and the not-yet-popular is necessary to maintain artistic vitality and growth. Our present musical, literary, and other classics were once contemporary, unorthodox, and experimental. Only by the testing and criticism attendant upon repeated reading and listening was there gradual selection of those that have survived as classics. Following our assumption, then, society has a double concern with communication of the artist's products: an interest in the full enjoyment of the classical heritage and an interest in keeping open the springs of creation which replenish the main stream of culture. In their understandable concern for the mass market, the agencies of public communication contribute much more adequately to the first interest than to the second.

THE NEWNESS OF NEWS   Superficially in contradiction to the preference of the mass media for long-established, generally approved opinions, prejudices, and tastes is their tendency to stress newness in reporting the day's happenings. Evidently interest in the news of the hour, however unpleasant or disturbing, is very widespread. Often this interest is almost independent of learning what is most significant in the flow of events. The popular desire is ministered to with great zeal and ingenuity by news gatherers and distributors. They have developed the news function into a highly competitive game which yields rich results in furnishing the public with full, uncensored access to a kaleidoscope of current items and activities. On the other hand, they have developed canons of selection which rule out as not newsworthy that which has occurred outside narrow limits of recency.

Indeed, preoccupation with the facts, ideas, and problems of the moment is a characteristic of all the commercial agencies of public communication. It centers their efforts on immediate sale and consumption of the current product with almost no machinery for preserving valuable contemporary items for later use. As a result, the newspaper of day before yesterday, last night's radio program, the magazine of two months ago, last year's popular novel or motion picture are often unobtainable through the regular commercial channels of distribution. Furthermore, neither in city dwellings and bookstores nor on newsstands are there more than the most meager facilities for storing the products of current mass communication for future use.

VOLUME AND DEADLINES   Concentration upon events and interests of the moment, for consumption at the moment, moreover, has involved the commercial media in the competitive production of an enormous quantity of material against frequent deadlines. The inevitable result is an average level of product far below that of which the participants would be capable if they were under less rigorous demands for volume and speed. Neither genius nor even talent is indefinitely expansible. Comedians who in the past have prepared a single finished program for a season in vaudeville must somehow fabricate a different performance each week for the radio. Commentators and columnists of long experience and rich background who given time for thought and study are capable of making valuable interpretations of public affairs in one or more fields must pontificate five times a week concerning the whole gamut of domestic and foreign events. Thus, the huge current output of material in the agencies of mass communication necessarily varies so greatly in quality that only a small part of it is worth preserving.[2] In this matter of huge volume of production against frequent deadlines it should be noted that book houses are in a very favorable position. Compared with the other mass media, theirs is a more deliberate, leisurely pace.

[2] It is estimated, for instance, that American AM broadcasting stations as a whole put 36,000 different programs on the air each day.

EXCEPTIONS TO MASS MEDIA CHARACTERISTICS   It needs to be
kept in mind that the special characteristics of commercial
communication described above—their emphases on celebrity
and stars, on personalizing, dramatizing, distorting, and sensationalizing, on majority opinion and tastes, on newness in
news, and their requirements of rapid, quantitative production
—are tendencies only, not invariable or universal rules. Among
the very large units, part of the output of most of them and
most of the output of some of them are clearly outside these
limitations of emphasis. Most of the special characteristics do
not apply at all to smaller communication units which in legal
form are commercial businesses, but actually are co-operative
ventures seeking to be self-supporting or are supported by
subsidies from memberships or contributions of one kind or
another. These smaller enterprises cater to all kinds of special
interests. Some are vigorous exponents of the dissenting, critical ideas of minorities. Others communicate facts and interpretations of an impersonal and undramatic character held by
their circle of subscribers to be important. Still others are outlets for the serious contemporary creators in literature and the
arts.

In some media, notably books and periodicals, such small
enterprises abound. In others, such as radio, theatrical motion
pictures, and television, they are almost nonexistent in the
sense of seeking audiences and interests which vary greatly
from the giant enterprises. This difference, of course, is significant for the public library, with its main stock in books and
periodicals.

THE EFFECTS OF THE NEWER MEDIA   The special emphases in
the content of the larger commercial units, together with their
huge daily output and wide coverage of the population, however, remain the major characteristics of present-day mass
communication. They have led many people to be concerned

about the total effect of the newer commercial media on national ideas, beliefs, and tastes. Some see, especially in the tabloids, comics, pulps, and slicks, in radio, motion pictures, and television, dangerous degenerative forces which are substituting popular clichés and mass prejudices for the discrimination and variety of individual judgments, the banalities and sentimentalities of untutored taste in music and art for progressively discriminating levels of appreciation, and crude, lurid pictures of crime and violence particularly unsuited to the sensitivity of children. Others, more hopeful, believe that these new instruments, wisely directed on behalf of sound social purposes, can lead the nation rapidly to greater racial tolerance, international understanding, the democratic virtues, and elevated tastes in music and the other arts.

MASS MEDIA AS INFORMATION AGENCIES   Quantitative studies of the actual effects on audiences of single items or programs of print, radio, or film seem to warrant neither the extreme hopes nor the fears expressed above. For imparting information each of the newer media is shown to be effective; but the effectiveness of each varies with the kind, complexity, and amount of information to be presented and the composition of the audience addressed. No one medium has established itself as superior for communicating knowledge of all kinds or for all audiences. If the different media are orchestrated in a combined effort to impart some specific body of information, they are likely to be more successful than if one medium alone is used for this purpose. A combination of a mass medium with face-to-face communication is shown to be very effective. Even combined efforts are sometimes ineffectual in producing significant results, however, when the audience aimed at must give voluntary attention. This is illustrated in a recent attempt in one American city to increase information, interest, and understanding with regard to the United Nations. The campaign was carried on for six months using newspapers, radio, motion pictures, public libraries, and other agencies of information.[3] Surveys of citizens at the beginning and end of the period indicated that the efforts of the media did not produce any significant effects. Such changes in knowledge, understanding, and interest as did occur appeared to be the results of events outside the community rather than of the local informational-educational program itself.

The same indications of the limited effectiveness of commercial mass media for imparting facts on a wide scale is seen more indirectly in the accumulating results of sample surveys to assess the information and understanding of citizens with regard to public affairs. The volume and the quality of the news, interpretation, and discussion of domestic and foreign issues made widely accessible over the past decade through American newspapers, magazines, books, radio, and motion pictures, represent an impressive achievement. Yet the polls of citizens over the same period reveal very meager results in the knowledge and understanding of these problems.

Surveys sampling citizen knowledge concerning the major issues in foreign affairs widely discussed in the mass media—such matters as the United Nations, the United States and Russia, the Marshall Plan, the Civil War in China, and the Atlantic Charter—show that percentages vary considerably with regard to the number of persons totally ignorant and those reasonably well informed concerning them. Putting the survey results together, however, they indicate that in general about one out of four adults tends to be informed on an issue

---

[3] See "Cincinnati Looks Again," a report of the effects of a six-month information program on behalf of the United Nations on interest, information, and opinion. National Opinion Research Center, University of Chicago, 1948 (mimeographed Report 37A); also, Shirley A. Star and Helen MacGill Hughes, "Report of an Educational Campaign: The Cincinnati Plan for the United Nations," *American Journal of Sociology*, LV (January, 1950), 389–400.

to the extent of being able to define terms and to give consistent, reasoned answers to questions concerning the issue. Sometimes, on such specific matters as naming the Four Freedoms or being able to describe what the Veto in the UN is, the informed group is as low as 10 percent. On other very general issues the informed percentage is as much as one third of those interviewed. There is an equally discernible tendency to report from 25 to 45 percent of those interviewed as being quite unaware of the problem about which they were queried ("never heard of it") and unable to define it or to give reasoned answers concerning it. The percentages reported here apply to general knowledge of major issues—what may be called the bare essentials of major problems. The proportion of persons ignorant of specific details of important public matters is, of course, higher. Between the recurring one quarter of adults who are reported to be well informed on major issues and the quarter to half who are ignorant and unaware of the issues there is a varying percentage of adults who are aware of the problems but uninformed or poorly informed with regard to them. On domestic issues the polls show the average percentage of informed adults to be about 5 percent higher; but the group of those both unaware and uninformed remains about the same as on foreign issues.[4]

Just what significance we should attach to these percentages is not evident. We do not know whether the percentage of citizens informed on public affairs is more or less than it was a generation or a century ago. We do not know whether it is more or less than in other countries operating as political democracies. We do not know what the danger point of ignorance is, below which the transaction of public business by the

[4] It should be borne in mind that these figures represent central tendencies only, not exact percentages typical of all polls, all sections of the country, all ages or degrees of schooling, or of both sexes. Breakdowns for all these factors reveal significant differences in the percentages of the ignorant and the informed.

democratic process is likely to fail. But it is clear that the extension of information to adults on public issues by the mass media on a vast scale does not by itself achieve general knowledge and understanding of those issues.

MASS MEDIA AND CHANGE OF ATTITUDES AND TASTES   Detailed studies of instances in which the mass media are seeking to alter personal attitudes, opinions, motivations, or tastes have yielded even more modest results than when they seek to impart information. Some reported studies, which measure effects produced by exposure to a single motion picture, radio program, book, article, or newspaper campaign, show changes so near to zero that they cannot be considered significant. There are other instances in which exposure to a communicated item or program designed to change opinion shows some modification in the opinions of the audience. There are the spectacular cases of persuasion by the Orson Welles *Message from Mars* program which misled many people into near-panic, and the Kate Smith marathon bond drive which achieved very large results in sales during and immediately following the broadcast. But the recorded changes, for the most part, are modest in amount, moving along a scale from a position at one end to a point nearer the center, or similar linear movements some distance along the line. When the persons addressed do not hold definite attitudes with regard to a subject matter, the effect of persuasion is measurable. But very few of the measured changes produced by the impact of mass media indicate conversion of opinion from pro to con or vice versa. There are instances in which taste for serious music among radio listeners seems to have been increased. These, however, were listeners who were already conditioned to be receptive to serious music by influences other than radio.

Evidently attitudes, opinions, motivations, and fundamental tastes are deeply rooted in the individual personality. They have their probable origin in the face-to-face influences of home, neighborhood, and school; they are strengthened or modified in adulthood by similar associations connected with occupational and other groups, and in sharply experienced events, such as war or involuntary unemployment. Whether exposure to a long-continued stream of mass communication, say four, five, or ten years of reading a tendentious magazine or newspaper, would become so much a part of a person's immediate environment as to approximate the influence of neighborhood groups has not been determined by any studies which have come to our attention. Such an influence, however, seems very likely.

The body of attitudes built up slowly over the years prevents a person from presenting an open mind to the succession of items, facts, and ideas coming to him through print, radio, or film. His existing attitudes provide an automatic device for self-selection among the volume of accessible material. What he has been accustomed to he likes and listens to; he reads what in advance he thinks he will approve. What might challenge his beliefs or prejudices is not read, is slighted in the reading, or if attended to is transformed by selection to fit into his existing pattern of attitudes and opinions. Because of self-selection also, a person's taste in entertainment or art is not at the mercy of the mass media. People seek out the material which is at the level of their interest and preference. Except for an occasional accident of contact, the other material does not come into the range of attention.[5]

[5]Just how far self-selection and personal preference serve to prevent the plethora of words, pictures, and ideas which assail the individual each day from confusing and bewildering him we cannot say on the basis of any reliable evidence. In the writings of expert students of mass communication there recurs an hypothesis that plethora, especially the plethora of exciting amusement and escape from reality, increases political apathy. But others, especially the practitioners of the mass communication arts, believe that the modern abundance of public report and discussion decreases political apathy. There are no quantitative studies to substantiate either hypothesis.

The available evidence, then, indicates that in spite of the huge volume and the great reach of the commercial agencies of public communication their actual effect on opinion, attitude, and belief, as well as on factual knowledge, is limited. Apparently in most cases the commercial agencies serve popular interests more than transform them, reinforce widespread attitudes and opinions rather than reverse them. The more decisive influences on motivation, belief, and attitude still seem to lie within the realm of more direct and intimate communication, including the intensive relationship of family and occupational groups and of organized education.[6]

THE PUBLIC LIBRARY'S NATURAL AUDIENCE   In the light of the incompleteness of the task of communication as performed by the commercial agencies we can begin to discern the natural and appropriate role of the public library in our society. Apparently it is not to attempt to compete with the commercial agencies on their terms, but rather to provide the kinds and qualities of service that those agencies are not equipped to give.

The audience for the public library thus is defined as numerically different from the maximums aimed at by the commercial media. Learning outside of school (indeed, much of learning in school that survives the forgetting process) depends upon the learner's interest, will, and ability to learn, as well as his opportunity to learn. Just what proportion of adults at any time have that will and ability is as yet undetermined. We know that it is much less than all adults or the 90–95 percent of adults who listen to programs of some sort on the radio and

[6]Some members of the Inquiry's Advisory Committee, after reviewing the staff reports of studies of effects of the media of mass communication believe that the interpretation of them presented here is overcautious. They feel that there have been observable effects of motion pictures on style and fashion, and of the mass media combined on public attitudes toward Germany in the last war and toward Russia today.

read some parts of a newspaper. Probably 10 percent of the whole number are illiterate or are incapable of learning through reading because of age or physical infirmity. There is a larger percentage—no one knows exactly how large—who innately lack the capacity to deal with abstract concepts, who cannot generalize beyond a very limited point, and for whom reading has a severely limited utility. And there is a third group, also of undetermined size in any community, who through lack of early opportunity or from long-established habit or personal bent have little or no serious concern with the world outside their immediate daily surroundings. Almost all these groups are reached in one way or another by the commercial agencies of public communication. But the communications to which they attend are obvious amusements, sports, and other entertainments, rather than material designed for serious personal enrichment or enlightenment.[7] This situation is not likely to be changed quickly or easily.

The three groups defined above make up a large proportion, but by no means all, of the 60 percent of adults in the present population whose schooling ended with the grammar grades (many persons of good or excellent intellectual ability, we know do not continue into high school or college, because of lack of educational facilities available to them in their community or for lack of personal funds to finance further schooling). They form part of the two thirds of the adult population who, as the Army Classification tests indicate, are not mentally equipped to complete an advanced liberal arts or professional education. They include a large proportion of the

[7]Nothing in this general analysis of the function of mass communication is meant to imply that furnishing entertainment, relaxation, and escape to people is unimportant. There is every indication that in our society such communication meets important human needs. The suggestion here is that the commercial media are equipped to meet that need in very large part, and that there are other social needs to which they do not minister with any adequacy.

37 percent of adults who in our survey of a national citizen sample have never used a public library. They constitute a large part of the 25 to 30 percent of adults reported above as unaware and ignorant of current public issues. And they contribute a large share of the 50 percent who on the average do not vote at elections even for such an important official as President of the United States.[8]

Indeed, as the quantitative studies show, lack of awareness or ignorance with regard to public issues and nonvoting correlate positively with lack of formal schooling. And we find that this same positive correlation exists between the lack of formal schooling and adult use of the public library: four times the percentage of all college graduates compared with the percentage of all those with only a grade school education are enrolled as regular public library patrons.

It would seem, then, that the public library's natural role as an agency of public communication is to serve the group of adults whose interest, will, and ability lead them to seek personal enrichment and enlightenment. The enlargement of this natural public library audience may well be the library's concern in co-operation with other agencies of education. But if our analysis is correct, the process of enlargement is slow, requiring intensive efforts and not producing numerically spectacular results. Meantime, adequate services to the existing and potential group of natural library users have a social value much greater than the gross numbers involved. For the public library's users, although they include persons of all kinds, degrees, and conditions, are not a cross section of the general population. As a group, they have had more schooling, have

[8]At the most recent Presidential election, 1948, the proportion of eligible voters who did not vote was approximately 49 per cent. And the average percentage of nonvoters in the Presidential elections since 1912 has been 40 to 50. In some states and localities and for some elections the extent of voting participation rises to 80 percent of those eligible; in other places and at other times the percentage falls as low as 10.

larger home libraries, read more magazines, see more movies, and listen to more of the serious radio programs than the average of all adults. They contain more than a numerical proportion of those who serve voluntarily on all levels as leaders of opinion and culture in their communities.

The obvious fact of widely distributed group leadership, leadership voluntarily delegated and accepted, and freely changed, is an inevitable part of the social texture of American communities in our day. The public library's users are only one manifestation of this basic fact. The very mass of mass communication, combined with the complexity and variety of public problems requiring political decision, creates a practical situation which makes the goal of universal citizen knowledge of public affairs doubtful. Today a man or a woman devoting full time and exceptional talent to current public problems can hope in his lifetime for mastery of no more than a tiny segment of the whole area of civic knowledge. But John Q. and Mary X. Citizen must do more than vote. They must devote a major portion of their time to earning a living, baking their daily bread, bringing up children, and having fun. Self-education on civic questions must, for all except a small minority, remain a spare-time job. The early nineteenth-century concept of the omnicompetent citizen has become an absurdity in our day.

Fortunately, the democratic process does not require a universal, equal acceptance of the burden of obtaining and digesting information and weighing ideas on current affairs. In the face of the impossible task of examining all the material and all the issues, most of us voluntarily delegate analysis and leadership in making decisions to people whom we trust. We choose these people freely, and we change our choices at will. The widespread network of opinion leadership is quite unofficial, informal, and flexible. Some persons have circles of influence in one field, others have influence with a small group on most subjects. Any citizen may be both a follower and a leader—a leader for three or four or ten people and a follower of a leader whose counsel affects a dozen, a hundred, a thousand, or several millions. In one New England village where the subtle process of influence and discipleship was plotted out in detail, the village barber and a banker's widow were found to be the most widely-accepted leaders of opinion. But usually these opinion leaders are not identified or catalogued. They are very numerous; leadership is exercised at some level by as many as one out of six, eight, or ten adults. Opinion leaders can be reached surely with information and ideas only by making the information and ideas available to everybody. This means keeping the public library's services open to all who seek them, but recognizing that those who habitually use them may be much less than a majority.

What is true of public affairs is equally true in the fields of science, literature, art, and music. The pursuit of these interests in any community is open to all, but their intensive cultivation is carried on by self-selected and changing minorities, small or large. The whole community's cultural interests are served indirectly by excellent service to these groups. The public library's concept of audience starts with a definition of services of positive personal and social value and seeks maximum quality and maximum audiences for these services.

THE LIBRARY'S APPROPRIATE SERVICES   Our review of the characteristics of the commercial agencies indicates that they leave undone or slight the performance of communication services which are indispensable for the health of our society. The unperformed tasks would seem to constitute the uniquely appropriate functions for noncommercial agencies of communication, of which the public library is one. They are:

1. To serve as centers for contemporary materials selected from each year's output by the judgment of experts as the

most reliable and authoritative, including artistic products of merit as determined by competent critics; and the promotion of the use of such materials by all available means.

2. To serve as centers where materials selected to give adequate and balanced representation to new, critical, often unpopular ideas, and to the preclassical, contemporary, unusual, and experimental in the arts can be brought into full use.

3. To serve as centers for the selection, organization, and promotion of the use of materials which are not new, but of great current relevance because of their enduring quality.

4. To serve as centers of selection, collection, and organization of the whole range of valuable materials in the form of print, picture, record, and film, in such a way as to focus the full resources of record quickly and easily on a particular subject or problem for those seeking such a service.

These four functions are not likely to be performed adequately or at all by the commercial media, characterized as they are by large volume and maximum coverage of the population. It is clear that the functions are not justified by the numbers of people reached so much as by the socially-valuable interests which they serve. They are functions which are made more rather than less necessary by the very flood of materials produced and distributed by commercial means. They seem, moreover, to be functions especially appropriate for performance by the library as a public institution.

THE OFFICIAL OBJECTIVES AND THE APPROPRIATE SERVICES   If we turn back to compare this definition of appropriate function arrived at by our survey of the whole machinery of public communication with the public library's own statements of historic faith and current official objectives, it seems evident that the librarians have been on the right track in describing their purposes. With some differences in phraseology, the librarian's definitions of objectives, with their emphasis on assembling and organizing educational materials, guidance and stimulation in their use, serving as a center of reliable information, freedom of access to reliable information on all sides of controversial questions, and giving people an opportunity to improve their capacity for appreciation and production in cultural fields, are in essential agreement with the four functions deduced from the general analysis of the business of communication. The official library objectives thus seem to mark the almost inevitable road for public libraries to follow if they are to play their appropriate role as a public agency of communication.

It remains to be seen how adequate the present public libraries are in structure, services, organization, support, operational procedures, and personnel to perform the functions they have marked out for themselves. This will be the subject of inquiry in succeeding chapters.

4

LIBRARY UNITS AND STRUCTURE

IT IS IMPOSSIBLE TO DESCRIBE the typical American public library. When we attempt to do so by locating the mid point on a numerical scale of library sizes, budgets, or books, we come up with a small building open to the public about a third of the day and evening hours per week, manned by one or two persons, in a town with a population of 2,500–3,000, a budget of less than $2,500, and a book stock of less than 10,000 volumes. This description tells us nothing about the much larger city library systems whose organization and problems occupy most of the attention in the deliberations of professional librarians and whose services have become the object of praise and emulation by librarians in other countries. The fact is that our public libraries vary so widely in size, resources, and facilities that for practical purposes their differences are those of kind as well as of degree.

THE FOUR PUBLIC LIBRARY TYPES   In our studies, therefore, we have found it most meaningful to divide the whole number of public libraries into four major groups. This scheme is somewhat arbitrary. One could break down the four types into at least two groups each, and we have done so for some purposes. The eight or nine resulting groups are more homogeneous internally, but they are not so sharply distinguished from each other in their activities. Using size of population served, total library expenditures, or total book stock alone as a basis for classification yields a similar grouping under the four public library types. We have used all three categories for purposes of analysis. But because size of population served has been employed most frequently in the library literature, we have adopted it as the primary basis for grouping the libraries into types.

The distribution of public libraries (including county as well as municipal institutions) in the country as a whole according to each of the three categories is as follows:[1]

POPULATION SERVED

	Population	Number of Libraries	Percentage of All Public Libraries
I	Over 100,000	135	2
II	25,000–100,000	577	8
III	5,000– 25,000	1,888	25
IV	Under 5,000	4,808	65
	Total	7,408	

TOTAL LIBRARY EXPENDITURES

	Annual Expenditure	Percentage of All Public Libraries
I	Over $100,000	2
II	$25,000–$100,000	4
III	$ 4,000–$ 25,000	23
IV	Under $4,000	71

TOTAL BOOK STOCK

	Total Number of Volumes	Percentage of All Public Libraries
I	150,000 or more	2
II	25,000–150,000	11
III	6,000– 25,000	43
IV	Less than 6,000	44

[1]The figures are derived from *Biennial Surveys of Education, Public Library Statistics, 1944-45*, issued by the United States Office of Education, reporting returns from 81 percent of American public libraries. Branches of city libraries were not listed separately. Branches of county libraries with their own local books and budgets, however, were separately listed. The figures given here are estimates of size of population served, library expenditures, and book stocks for the whole number of public libraries, arrived at by adding the proportionate number of libraries not replying to each of the size groups that did reply. This method probably results in overestimating

On the basis of these figures and from our analyses of public libraries in our sample, especially the studies of their personnel and technical processes, we have defined the four groups as follows:

Type I: Large city libraries (over 100,000 population), totaling 2 percent of the country's public libraries. They have annual expenditures of $100,000 or more, ten or more branches depending on city size, a book stock of 150,000 volumes as a minimum, and a total personnel, including many specialists, numbered in the hundreds. They have highly organized and professionally manned departments, with highly organized and important reference and bibliographical activities, along with extensive circulation, children's and school departments, and other special services. These libraries are open all day and evening, six or six and a half days each week.

Type II: Smaller city libraries (25,000–100,000 population), totaling 8 percent of the whole number of public libraries. Their expenditures range from $100,000 down to $25,000; in a minority of cases they are below that amount. They have a book stock of from 25,000 to 150,000 volumes, and are open on a full six-day schedule of sixty-one to seventy-two hours. They have three to ten branches and a personnel of fifteen or more. They have definitely organized and professionally led reference and children's departments along with extensive circulation activities, usually with supervisors of major operations instead of highly specialized department heads.

Type III: Town and large village libraries in places with 5,000–25,000 population, totaling 25 percent of the country's public libraries. These libraries have annual budgets ranging from less than $4,000 to $25,000, and a book stock numbering 6,000 to 25,000 or more. They are open twenty-five to sixty

---

the number of libraries in the larger groups, this because of the likelihood that of those not replying most were very small libraries without adequate clerical facilities.

hours a week only, with a staff of three as a minimum including a professional library head and general assistants, often trained to do book selection, reference, and children's work. The reference work usually consists of aid to school students and clubs as well as the handling of individual informational queries.

Type IV: Small village libraries with populations less than 5,000, totaling 65 percent of the public libraries in the United States. Their annual expenditures are under $4,000. Their book stock ranges from a few shelves of books for circulation to as many as 10,000 volumes; two thirds of them have less than 6,000 volumes. They are open on a part-time basis from a few hours up to twenty-four hours a week, with a single part-time librarian, in most cases not professionally trained in a library school, aided by a part-time, nonprofessional assistant. They carry on very little reference work and have no departmental organization.

PUBLIC LIBRARY COVERAGE   This pattern of public libraries is a natural consequence of the universal practice in the United States of considering the public library a local function to be initiated by local effort, with its financial support entirely from the local government and its control deriving from the municipal governing authority. Because the largest number of government units in the United States consist of small villages and towns, the largest number of public libraries—approximately two thirds of the whole number—are in small towns and villages. If we add to them the sizable groups of libraries in towns of 5,000 to 25,000 population, they comprise nine tenths (6,700) of the country's public library units.

The numerical preponderance of the small library units does not mean that they provide the public library service received by most of the people. The Type IV small town and village units, though two thirds of the whole number of public libraries, serve directly only a little more than one tenth of the population receiving library service. The city libraries (Types I and II), on the other hand, serve directly approximately half the population receiving any library service, although these libraries constitute only 10 percent of the whole number of public libraries.

Indeed, the device of organizing public libraries by local initiative and under local control is inadequate for creating libraries at all in many small municipal units. Whereas all the cities of 40,000 or more have libraries, 96 percent of the municipalities with a population from 10,000 to 40,000 and 95 percent of the towns with a population of 4,000 to 10,000 have direct public library service, only about one third of the 14,500 villages in the United States with populations less than 5,000 have, as yet, organized and maintained independent public libraries. This means that the principle of locally-created, autonomous municipal library units has led to the provision of libraries in less than half the municipalities of the country.

Furthermore, public library service defined as a function of incorporated municipal units fails to reach the more than one third of the nation's population (approximately forty-eight million according to the 1940 census) who live outside cities, towns, and villages, in unincorporated rural territory.

THE COUNTY LIBRARIES   These two inherent deficiencies in the coverage of the municipal library system, that is, its inability to include either the smallest municipalities or the unincorporated rural areas, began to be appreciated by library leaders nearly half a century ago. They initiated the so-called library extension movement which took the form of establishing public libraries under county support and control. In some states, where very few local libraries existed previously, a single public library at the county seat has been instituted. In others, a central headquarters for the county library has been established, with branches and stations in villages, hamlets, schools, or crossroads centers within the county or with bookmobile service to such places.

The library extension pioneers who counted on total county populations and tax resources as the basis on which to build the county libraries, however, have been disappointed. State legislators were willing to empower county boards or the county electorate to establish public libraries if they wished to, but they were not willing to have the county absorb village, town, or city libraries within the county unless these units decided by formal action to be absorbed. In a few instances existing city and town libraries have been completely incorporated voluntarily as units of the county library. In a number of counties municipal libraries within the county have been tied in by contract to render part of or all the county's library service. But in most cases the municipal libraries, particularly the larger ones, have chosen to remain outside the county system as independent library enclaves surrounded by county library service. What has resulted in many places, then, is small county libraries serving the residue of population outside the more populous centers. It was evident in our observation of the areas in our sample, moreover, that in the case of several of the urban libraries that contracted to render county service the library board and management have centered their attention mainly on urban needs, so that the county service is inferior or, at least, subsidiary. Whatever were the objectives of those who secured the state enabling acts for county libraries, the result has not been in most cases to create single library systems in each county large enough to provide modern library service.

The addition of county libraries has, it is true, extended public library coverage in the strict geographical sense. About one fourth of the 3,069 counties in the United States have established a county library of some sort. The number of people outside the direct-service area of any public library is thereby reduced from forty-eight million to approximately thirty-five million, 91 percent of whom live in unincorporated areas. The unserved group, however, still comprises as much as one quarter of the total national population.

Like municipal libraries, which vary in size from those in tiny villages to the libraries in great cities, county libraries vary greatly in size and population. The distribution of county library populations can be seen from the following figures showing percentages in each of the four public library types:

COUNTY LIBRARIES IN THE UNITED STATES

Size of Population Served	Percentage of County Libraries
100,000 and over	3
25,000–100,000	44
5,000– 25,000	43
Under 5,000	10

As compared with public libraries as a whole, there are fewer county libraries in Type IV, but more than two fifths are in the 5,000–25,000 group, and only 3 percent serve populations of 100,000 or more. In total expenditures, as the following figures reveal, they show an even closer approximation to the whole group of public libraries, with few budgets (8 percent) over $25,000 and only 20 percent with more than 25,000 volumes in their collections.

COUNTY LIBRARIES IN THE UNITED STATES

Total Expenditures	Percentage of County Libraries	Total Volumes in Book Stock	Percentage of County Libraries
$100,000 and over	1.5	100,000 and over	4
$ 25,000–$100,000	6.5	25,000–100,000	16
$ 5,000–$ 25,000	41	5,000– 25,000	54
Under $5,000	51	Under 5,000	26

The major result, then, of the county library movement has been to increase the number of small public libraries serving small populations with small stocks of books. The vast

majority of counties in the United States, like the majority of municipal corporations, are too small in population
and resources to provide modern public libraries. There are
great variations between the states and the regions in numbers, sizes, and populations of counties, from a Texas county
with 285 inhabitants to Cook County, Illinois, with 3,000,000
people; a Rhode Island county with an area of twenty-four
square miles to a California county with 20,000 square miles;
the states of Massachusetts and Connecticut, with 13 and 8
counties, respectively, to Texas with 254, Georgia with 159,
and Kentucky with 120 counties apiece. More significant,
most of the counties in the country contain only 10,000—
30,000 people each, less than the minimum as defined in a later
chapter for supporting adequate library service. Only 6 percent of the counties have a population of more than 100,000.
More than half the 6 percent are essentially urban areas served
by large city libraries. Probably not more than one in twenty
counties outside these urban areas has a population large
enough to justify the creation of an independent library system.

Small units in close contact with potential library users are
part of any public library system. Especially in the Southern
states, where the county is the ultimate unit of local government, building county libraries has been a counterpart to the
earlier creation of town and village libraries in the Northeast
and Middle West. Both types of small units are necessary in a
total library structure. But because of their size and resources
and the difficulty of unifying the library services within their
territory, the counties, like municipalities, are inherently incapable of providing complete, modern library service in line
with official public library objectives. As will be seen below,
library leaders more and more generally conceive of the small
library units as local distribution centers connected with
larger units, together possessing total resources, adequate per-

sonnel, book stock, and other materials, to provide complete modern service.

Out of the county library movement have come examples of these larger public library units for rural areas. In several states, but particularly in California, there are counties large enough in area, population, and tax resources to maintain a modern library service. In some of them, county libraries have been created which include all or nearly all the cities and villages within their borders. They have appropriations and book stocks which put them in the Type I (130 largest cities) public libraries. They have professional staffs with specialized skills furnishing guidance and direct services to scores of branches located throughout the county. Many of the branches were independent village libraries formerly and retain much of the local loyalty and special character of such institutions.

These rural equivalents of medium and large city libraries may be the prototypes of modern public library organization for both urban and rural areas. Like the city library, the large county library operates on two levels, with a main library serving as a book, reference, and administrative center and a number of branches and other small units. The central library carries on all the technical processes connected with book selection, accessioning, cataloguing, repairing, storing, and discarding. The books constitute a common stock centrally catalogued and circulated so as to afford maximum use. In some counties films, music, and other recordings are also catalogued as single collections to be circulated among the branches and stations. The headquarters staff conducts a central reference service for the whole county system. Staff specialists in technical processes, in work with children, in work with adult groups, and in audio-visual materials are on the road much of the time, aiding the branch librarians in these aspects of the service to their little communities. Needless to say, the distribution of local library units over many miles of open country presents transportation, communication, and administrative problems unknown in urban systems. But in our sample we observed that these problems are being met successfully in some counties where the most distant branch is fully a hundred miles from the headquarters library.

The library extension leaders who have accepted the concept of units like those described above have actually rejected the county as the universal unit for rural library organization. Even in California where large county libraries developed early as models for emulation, some of the counties lack the population and tax income considered adequate for full, modern library service. In a number of those with adequate total resources, one or more cities have refused to cast in their lot with the county library system, and other cities having contracts with county libraries leave much to be desired in the way of adequate service.

REGIONAL AND DISTRICT LIBRARIES   In moving toward larger units, however, proponents of library extension still rely mainly on the county as a base for organization rather than create special *ad hoc* districts which disregard county lines. In a number of states acts have been passed enabling two or more counties to vote themselves into a multi-county regional or district library unit. The political process involved is even more difficult than for the establishment of a unified county library. There must be simultaneous persuasion of two or three adjoining counties to throw in their facilities and tax money to an inter-county authority of which they are only a part. And the new entity will not achieve its possibilities if at the same time the larger town and city libraries within the counties have not affiliated themselves with their county libraries. The enabling acts, moreover, permit a county by popular vote or vote of its governing board to withdraw from, as well as to join, a region or district so that the newly established library agency seems to be a kind of uneasy alliance which may dissolve with a shift of political sentiment in any one of its constituent parts. Nevertheless, despite the political hazards and due largely to very skillful and persistent leadership on the part of the state library officials, a few intercounty regions have been established with staff and appropriations of adequate size for effectual public library service.

Meantime, in two New England states, and on an experimental basis for one area in New York, the state itself has set up library regional service centers to supplement and aid the local public libraries within their regional borders. And in states as dissimilar and widely separated as Connecticut, Wisconsin, and New Mexico state-created library regions have been proposed in recent official surveys of library needs.

There are some obvious formal differences between the library regions constituted by state action and those brought into being by concurrent local action. Regions created by state statute or administrative act may have boundaries which follow natural trading areas rather than county lines, or they may be assimilated to state regions created for other purposes. The state-created regional center provides an auxiliary service only to the public libraries within the region. It has no legal authority over them. Each local library retains full legal authority over its personnel, is under its own board of trustees, may buy its own books, and with its own funds may carry on its own special services. It accepts voluntarily, and later may refuse, the aid, guidance, and special services of the regional library center. It may continue to live in the region as an independent library enclave, like many city and town libraries now in county systems. The region created by concurrent county votes, on the other hand, is the public library authority for the villages, towns, cities, and counties that have voted themselves in. What were local or county libraries are transformed legally into branches of the regional library, with the local library personnel and services subject to the regional library authority. In one case the authority is transferred from a smaller to a larger local area; in the other, the local authority remains intact, but the local services are augmented by aid provided in defined regions by the state library authority.

As we observed the two systems in operation, however (and there are very few examples to observe as yet), the distinctions between them seemed to be more of a legal than of a functional nature. In both, the regional center is engaged mainly in buying and circulating books and other materials among local libraries, in carrying on the technical processes involved in acquisition and cataloguing for the local libraries and in providing guidance by its specialized personnel to local librarians not professionally trained for library tasks. The towns and counties in a self-constituted region who vote themselves into the larger system may later vote themselves out, just as libraries in a state-constituted region may accept or reject the regional services. The headquarters staff in both systems, therefore, seemed equally solicitous about respecting local autonomy, local differences, and institutional pride. The local libraries which have become regional branches looked and acted very much like local libraries. In some, the library board was retained as an advisory group; in practically all, the existing library staff members continued at their posts as branch librarians. Fundamentally, both systems depend upon the maintenance of voluntary local co-operation. In operational terms they are library confederations rather than federations.

In time even the formal distinction between the two systems may become blurred. This would happen if for a demonstration period, or permanently, state-constituted regional centers should furnish direct library service on a free or contract basis to localities in the region which have no libraries of their own. Such regions would then include branches, stations, and bookmobiles as well as independent but co-operating local libraries. It would happen, also, if state aid to self-constituted regions should be given in terms of books and loan of skilled personnel rather than general money grants and if regional library boards should assume an active role in planning and sponsorship of the library service in the region.

The minimum size considered adequate for regional library units has been much discussed among extension librarians. The American Library Association, by promulgating "standards," has set up minimum figures for an adequate library service in terms of total annual expenditures. Although among librarians they tend to be accepted as scientifically established norms, they are really averages of annual expenditures in good libraries at current price levels. Their topical character is revealed in the perspective of a decade or two during which the ALA "standards" of expenditure changed from $6,000 to $25,000 to $37,500 to $60,000.[2]

As will be seen in Chapter 8, the studies of the Inquiry lead to a definition of adequacy of a public library unit in terms of numbers and kinds of staff members, and of types and quantities of new materials needed to provide a modern library service. At present price levels for salaries and library materials we found the dividing line between adequacy and inadequacy in our sample at or near $100,000 total expenditures. The total includes services or materials available for the general pool, whether contributed by a constituent local library or the regional center. Economy in operation would dictate full use in any region of existing city libraries for headquarters and payments to such libraries for contribution of their skilled personnel, technical, and reference services to regional activity so as to avoid building separate staffs or facilities.

[2] The latter figure, $60,000, is Dr. Lowell Martin's revision of an earlier ALA estimate, further adjusted to more recent price levels.

METROPOLITAN LIBRARY REGIONS   Preoccupation with the problem of building larger service units for rural areas has drawn attention away from the inadequacy of the present public library structure in metropolitan areas. These large population units, of which there are more than a hundred in the country as a whole, with central foci for business, shopping, recreation, and possessing a local transportation network, are, in a socio-economic sense, single communities. Governmentally, however, they may be a mosaic of a half dozen to fifty or more separately organized municipal corporations or districts, each with its own governing body and administrative services. In addition, they usually contain patches of unincorporated territory, with public services of an attenuated character provided by one or more counties within the area.

The public library organization in metropolitan areas is a reflection of the general governmental pattern. A striking example was exposed to view recently by the survey of public libraries in the East Bay Area of the San Francisco region.[3] It showed an area with two and a half million population, having one of the country's highest averages of per capita wealth and education, comprising within its borders one of the country's largest universities and university libraries and a score of smaller institutions of higher education. It is an area that could readily provide every resident, through a federated library organization, with direct, easy access to the whole volume of current and standard books and other materials. Instead, each of the thirty-four towns and cities of the region has its own independent library system, with libraries supported by, and serving, populations ranging from 1,500 to 825,000. In addition, each of the region's eight counties has a library system with local branches or stations averaging sixty per county. Be-

[3]Joseph L. Wheeler, "A Regional Library Service for the East Bay Area" (mimeographed), Oakland, The East Bay Committee, 1948.

tween none of the municipalities or counties is there any planned library co-ordination. Technical processes are duplicated, books are idle, distribution of services is uneven, and funds are dissipated so that no part of the area has the completeness of resources and excellence of service which the whole region could have if it were organized as a co-ordinated metropolitan library system. The San Francisco region is an extreme example of unorganized urban library facilities. But within our sample and outside it we encountered other large urban areas with a similar multiplication of municipal services. In fact, in only two large cities coming under observation did we find that either by accident or foresight a sizable metropolitan region was served by a single public library system.

The problem of a library structural unit adequate for metropolitan regions, like the problem of a unit of adequate size for rural regions, is not one for public libraries only. For more than a generation both have been the primary concern also of persons engaged in performing the school, health, highway, welfare, and other local public services. And they are governmental problems not only in the United States but also in all other countries which have progressed from a horse-and-buggy, agricultural, and handicraft society to an industrial society with scientific-mechanized agriculture and with rapid, cheap transportation and communication. In such societies the problem of each public service is much the same as for the others: the need in sparsely settled areas to have a local unit large enough to make possible modern equipment and expert specialized personnel for direct service to consumers, and in large urban areas the need for a governmental-administrative unit of the same size and scope as the urban social community itself. By some, the creation of larger units in each case is viewed as centralization. More properly, it is the attempt to reconstitute and to vitalize local units in terms of the modern necessities for effective local administration.

In the case of a few functions in metropolitan areas, such as water supply, sewage disposal, docks and harbors, parks and boulevards, the waste and even danger of the municipal jig saw puzzle have led to creation of an *ad hoc* corporation, to provide one or another of these services for the whole metropolitan population. In the case of the public library, however, we encountered no case of this type of *ad hoc* consolidation in a metropolitan region. The nearest approaches to such action are the few instances in which there are a metropolitan union catalogue and agreements of the libraries in an urban area to avoid duplication in purchase of new books in special fields. There is, after all, not the same urgency for integrating public library service as some other functions, such as sewage and water supply, where one municipality's waste may pollute its neighbor's water supply or public bathing beach.

Even for the other services the *ad hoc* solution has grave handicaps. Although it usually gives effective results for the single service over the whole area, it tends to complicate the area's general government even further by adding one more governmental unit to those already existing. Some observers of this unco-ordinated, piecemeal approach to the problem of ultimate units for the local public services have concluded that the only satisfactory solution is transition to general units of local government large enough to perform the local functions with modern tools and personnel. For the public library this would mean participation as one of many services in enlarged, all-purpose local government. But after thirty years the program for larger all-purpose units remains an academic conception rather than an operating reality. It is difficult to say which is the more complete record of inaction—the failure to create larger ultimate units for the local public services outside the cities or the failure to effect metropolitan consolidation or federation. The governmental logic and administrative practicability of the proposals for larger ultimate units have stood the test of argument and criticism. Evidently there is needed analysis of the political process by which the change can be effected. This is the subject of Chapter 7.

STATE LIBRARIES   In addition to municipal, county, and regional libraries serving people directly, another stratum in the national public library structure consists of the state library and library extension agencies located in each of the forty-eight state capitals. The state library agencies, like municipal and county libraries, vary enormously in budgets, book stock, and personnel—from musty, poorly-organized, inadequate collections in charge of untrained librarians to large, well-housed central libraries with professional staffs exercising vigorous leadership among public libraries throughout the state. The latter are in the minority. All state libraries serve the legislative, administrative, and judicial officers of the state government. But in most of them one or more services are provided also to the public libraries in the state. Indeed, one traditional activity in some states serves the people directly. This is the lending of books by the state library (or a special circulating collection maintained by a separate library extension agency) by mail on request, in boxed lots, to local libraries, schools, clubs, or singly to individual citizens in places where there is no local public library.

The volume and quality of books lent in these ways differ greatly from state to state. In the more active state libraries direct circulation is no longer the center of its program; the tendency is to develop central reference in aid of local librarians rather than a general circulation service. Both are noted here to indicate that in a very superficial sense the citizens of a number of states have 100 percent public library service.

Another traditional service of the state library agency is the encouragement of the creation of public libraries in towns and villages throughout the state, more recently the promotion of county libraries and multi-county or regional libraries. Library statistics and a bulletin are published, conferences are promoted, speeches are made, and small grants of money are made to local libraries. In a few states grants in larger amounts are given to encourage the establishment and maintenance of county and multi-county units. As we have seen above, a small number of state library systems provide the funds for books and appoint the personnel for regional library centers, which in turn provide books, personnel, and technical services for libraries within the region.

For the most part, state library activities, aside from service to the officers of the state government, have been directed toward improvement of library service outside the major cities. This is probably due to the fact that cities have supplied their own lay and professional leadership for library development. In a number of state libraries this emphasis is reflected in the experience of the library staff in charge.

COLLEGE, UNIVERSITY, AND RESEARCH LIBRARIES   We should not end our description of public library units in the United States without mentioning other library agencies supported by public taxation which serve as auxiliary, at least, to the public library structure. There were, at the last count, some 1,728 libraries connected with institutions of higher education distributed widely in the various regions of the country. Over a thousand of them (1,067) are in colleges and universities, professional and technical schools. The others are in teachers' colleges, normal schools, and junior colleges. These academic libraries, like the public libraries, vary greatly in size, resources, and personnel. Many of the smaller ones are fully occupied in meeting the current needs of the faculty and students which they are built primarily to serve, and their collections contain little of special value for other users. But a considerable number have organized large and valuable collections of books and periodicals. Eight of the university libraries have more than a million volumes each; 133 other academic libraries have book stocks of more than 100,000 each. These larger libraries are similar in size and almost exactly match in number the larger public libraries, to be found in cities of more than 100,000 population. They represent an important public library resource, which is now available directly to university scholars and might be made more generally, though indirectly, available to serious students, scholars, and reference workers outside as well as inside universities and colleges.

Very similar to the large university libraries are a few independently endowed research libraries whose collections are available, with only minimum restriction, to scholars and reference workers generally. And in the same category are the federal government's libraries in Washington, especially the Library of Congress.

THE LIBRARY OF CONGRESS   The latter institution plays a dual role, as do the state libraries. Its primary commitment is to serve the information and research needs of the officers of the federal government, particularly the members of the legislative branch. In carrying on this function the Library of Congress has become one of the largest reference and research collections in the world. To organize its materials for use the Library has developed highly expert cataloguing and bibliographical personnel and activities, which have provided the basis for valuable services to the public and other libraries of the country.

These incidental but important services include the preparation, printing, and sale of catalogue cards and of the *Cumulative Catalog*, which make available to libraries at small cost an expertly catalogued card and reference list for every book currently published in the United States as well as other current publications acquired by the Library of Congress and a group of other large libraries co-operating with it. The Library also makes available on request the materials in its vast holdings to other libraries through photo-duplication and interlibrary loans. These and other research purposes are aided by the maintenance of a union catalogue of the holdings of a number of the nation's largest libraries. The Library is also active in preparing regular bibliographical guides and special bibliographies. More recently the Library has played an active role among the nation's research libraries in encouraging the allocation of the acquisition of the current book output of other countries and in joint bibliographical enterprises.

In these various ways the Library of Congress has become an essential part of the operating machinery of American public libraries. It has not acted as the national library or assumed a role in relation to state and local public libraries equivalent to those state library agencies which directly stimulate and guide local library developments. Its extra-federal functions are justified as by-products of its primary services to the agencies of the national government.[4] Nor has it acted as *the* nation's research and bibliographical center, but rather as one of the country's forty or fifty largest research libraries. Nevertheless, its services give it an important place in the public library structure of the United States.

SCHOOL LIBRARIES   Quite different from the university libraries and the Library of Congress are the many school libraries connected with public elementary and high schools. In sheer numbers these school library units probably equal the public libraries of the country. But even more than is true of the public libraries, most of them are very small in budgets and book stock and many are manned by part-time,

[4]There is a diminutive unit in the Office of Education which was originally designed to carry on Federal functions in stimulation and aid of state and local public libraries. As yet, however, this unit has been given no specific authority, funds, or personnel to engage in any such program.

inadequately-trained personnel. Their books are usually limited to immediate classroom use. Thus, they are in practice severely limited to serving a specific segment of the public: pupils within the public schools, and for this public they share library service with the public library in their communities. In a real sense, however, they are part of the nation's public library structure. They are supported from tax revenues, and they serve the public without charge.

SPECIAL LIBRARIES   Finally, there is a group of libraries, now more than 2,400, which it is not so easy to classify as part of the public library structure, namely, the special libraries organized to make information available to a particular organization or a limited group whether business, industrial, nonprofit, or governmental. Although they usually follow large industries when they are located in small places, special libraries tend to be concentrated in large cities more than are public or school libraries. In most cases special librarians are users of the public libraries in their communities and often establish co-operative working relations with them. In return, public libraries are frequently able to make the resources of special libraries available to qualified experts who are in search of special materials. Thus, to some extent special libraries, though primarily limited to a definite, private group, become informal auxiliaries to the reference service of public libraries.

THE NATURE OF THE PUBLIC LIBRARY STRUCTURE   Our summary indicates clearly that the main characteristic of the American public library structure is multiplicity of independent units. All units together do not provide complete coverage of the population. Moreover, the variation in their size and adequacy is such that there is no approach to equality of even minimum service. The multiplicity of independent units and the extreme variations in their size and adequacy are characteristic not only of municipal libraries, but also of county, state, school, college, and university libraries. Furthermore, the several kinds of library institutions in any community, region, or state—public, school, university, research, and special—have no organized, co-operative relationships with each other except for an occasional informal working agreement. This is true also of the public libraries in metropolitan areas. In brief, the United States has a multitude of libraries, some of them magnificent institutions, but it has no library system. It falls far short of providing the people everywhere equal access to the means of learning through the reading of books.

We are so accustomed to the present library structure that we do not recognize that it is only one way of providing a public service such as this. The essential features of the structure are a collection of books and other materials in self-contained library buildings owned by and serving the population which supports the particular library. It is the concept of the private home library writ large for the community. One can imagine a sharply different concept, in which individual public libraries did not own their books and other materials, but served as depositories for changing collections, each library being part of a community, regional, state, or even national pool of materials and the librarians in each unit serving as centers of information, reference, and procurement by loan. This would involve elaborate arrangements for priorities, allocations, and exchange between the libraries of a community or region. But it would make for complete coverage of the population and would come nearer to equality of service to the whole public.

Such interrelated or integrated machinery for a service of communication is not unknown in our society. From the very first, governmental provision through the Post Office for the distribution and exchange of newspapers, magazines, and personal correspondence has been organized to provide equal service to every person within the national borders. The post office building in the village street can easily be mistaken for the public library; its staff consists almost entirely of local citizens. But unlike public libraries, no local post office is independent; rather it is a related part of a single, national public monopoly. Similarly, the American telephone system is a highly integrated, near-monopoly, under private ownership and governmental regulation extending telephone communication on terms of equal service to almost every home in the land. Indeed, in the case of both postal and telephone services the integration and the interrelationship of service extend far beyond our national borders so that the lowliest and most isolated citizen can establish quick personal communication by mail or telephone with persons on the opposite side of the world.

This is not to suggest that public libraries should be drastically reconstituted as a single, integrated mechanism on a national, state, or even community level, in the interest of providing equal and complete service to the whole population. The comparison is made, rather, to indicate that the present pattern of extremely localized and unrelated public library units is only one way of organizing such a public service in a modern democratic state, not the only way, or necessarily the best way.

5

LIBRARY MATERIALS

PUBLIC LIBRARY RESOURCES in terms of books and other materials are determined to a large extent by the concept of public library functions held by the librarian and the library board. Their definition of services will be reflected in the kind and quality of annual purchases, and eventually the holdings of different classes of library materials: reference aids, children's literature, current and standard fiction and nonfiction, periodicals, pamphlets, recordings, films, and documents. Our studies have indicated, however, that materials are also directly dependent upon the size of the library and of its annual budget. Thus, public library organization in the United States has much to do with library operations. In a real sense, form has determined function in the public library field.

THE BOOK HOLDINGS   The relationship between library size and library materials can be seen in the reports of total book expenditures made to us by the libraries in the Public Library Inquiry sample. The Type I libraries in the sample, serving populations of 100,000 and more, purchased an average of 48,000 volumes in 1948. For libraries in this group the problem, as far as American publications are concerned, is mainly to determine what is not worth having and the number of duplicates to buy from the annual output of trade and general publications totaling approximately 5,000 volumes a year.

The average of total book purchases in the Type II libraries, serving populations of 25,000 to 100,000, was 4,800 in 1948, with a range from 1,560 to nearly 10,000 titles for libraries in this group. By careful selection most of these libraries also are able to acquire all but a small portion of the year's annual output of new books.

With regard to the Type III libraries (serving 5,000 to 25,000 population) it is a different story. The average of purchases in 1948 for the whole group was 1,650 volumes, with a range from 570 to 4,000 volumes purchased by libraries in the 10,000 to 25,000 population group and from 490 to 1,100 in the 5,000–10,000 group. Here the year's purchases are limited to only a fraction of current publications.

In the Type IV libraries (serving less than 5,000 population) the average number of books bought per library was 330, with a range from less than 200 to 460. This does not give the picture for the considerable number of very small public libraries in the villages of 1,000 population or less at the bottom of the scale. Recent surveys, such as that of public libraries in Connecticut, where there are many small village libraries, report that a third of the state's libraries average annual book purchases of less than 200 volumes.

What happens to book selection in libraries with such enormously different budget resources? Several studies of library book stocks indicate the results of the inability of smaller libraries to buy more than a small percentage selected from the whole range of books published. They become more completely circulating libraries than reference libraries; they tend to have more fiction than nonfiction in their collections; and, indeed, they are more collections of popular current fiction than anything else.

The Inquiry's information on purchases and holdings in its sample of sixty public libraries tends to reinforce the conclusion from other studies. The libraries were asked to check their holdings on six lists of the books published in 1948: the twelve fiction best sellers, the twelve "notable works" of the year's fiction as selected by an ALA committee of public librarians, twelve works of fiction selected by professional book critics as among the year's best in quality; also thirty each of (1) the year's nonfiction best sellers, (2) the librarians' list of "notable" nonfiction, and (3) the critics' consensus of best books as compiled by us from book reviews. Altogether, the lists comprised 125 titles, 2½ percent of the year's publication of trade and general books.

The returns from the libraries in the Inquiry sample[1] showed that the fiction best sellers were purchased by public libraries of all sizes: an average of 90 percent or more by libraries with total budgets of $10,000 and more, an average of 82 percent by libraries having less than that amount. In the case of the librarians' list of "notable" fiction, all the libraries but two with budgets over $50,000 a year had all the books on the list, and these two together had all but four of the listed books. The smaller libraries had most of the titles, those with budgets under $10,000 averaging three-quarters of the total list.

The list of current fiction chosen by critics for quality presents a different story. In the groups with $25,000 budgets and more the average holdings were 67 to 69 percent. But the average percentage held by the smaller libraries was $10,000–$25,000, 42 percent; $5,000–$10,000, 15 percent; $2,500–$5,000, 11 percent. On the critics' list was Cozzens' *Guard of Honor*, which received the Pulitzer Award as the year's best American novel some time after the libraries had checked the lists. All but one of the larger libraries (budgets over $25,000) had purchased the book; none of the libraries with budgets below $10,000 had done so.

The returns with regard to current nonfiction were similar in most respects to those for fiction. The books on the list of critics' choices were not held so widely by the larger libraries,

[1]Fifty-eight checked and returned the list. Two of the smaller libraries in the Inquiry sample failed to do so.

and only 2 percent, on the average, were held by the smallest groups (budgets under $10,000).

This and other available evidence indicates that the smaller public libraries select their current books on the basis of their sales volume even more than upon the recommendations made by leaders of their own profession and much more than upon the recommendations of professional critics. Considering the limited number of volumes which the majority of the small libraries are able to acquire each year they seem to have concluded that their most adequate, if not principal, service is as a library of popular current fiction and nonfiction.

The public library's acknowledged function, however, has always included the assembly of other than current books, especially of standard works of authority in the various fields of knowledge. In order to get some indication of book resources in this area, the Inquiry sent to the sample libraries several lists, totaling 230 titles of books for general readers in fields of serious adult interest. They were selected by experts in each of several fields and included the following subjects: United States history, government and politics, labor, science and society, food and nutrition, photography, education for family life.

Returns from the sample libraries for these lists were much the same as for current publications. Public libraries with budgets of more than $100,000 had on their shelves 50 to 99 percent of the titles listed; the libraries in the $25,000–$100,000 group held a quarter to a half of them; the holdings of the $10,000–$25,000 group averaged one quarter of these titles; the libraries below $10,000 averaged 0 to 11 percent of the books on the lists. In United States history the average was 10 percent in the smallest libraries; for the how-to-do-it books, 5 percent; for the public affairs list, 3 percent. The returns indicated, then, that two thirds of the public libraries in the United States, that is, those serving populations of less than 5,000, make no serious attempt to build collections of popular but reliable reference works in major areas of serious adult interests.

PERIODICAL AND NEWSPAPER HOLDINGS   In addition to collecting and lending books, practically all public libraries subscribe to a number of current periodicals, some of which are later bound for use by their patrons. Although a long-established service, the provision of periodicals for public use is by no means so large or so important a part of library activity as is the purchase and lending of books. This phenomenon may result in part from the fact that the commercial distribution of magazines, both by subscription and by newsstand sale, makes them more easily accessible than does the commercial distribution of books. At any rate, surveys of magazine readers show that an average of only 2 to 3 percent of them obtain their magazines from the public library.

The policy of selecting magazines differs somewhat from that evident in choosing books. There is a whole group of periodicals whose readers are numbered by millions—especially younger people, the public library's largest users. These are the romance, love, adventure, mystery, pulp, movie and radio magazines, and the comics. Yet in our sample practically no libraries subscribed to more than one of them, and most libraries subscribed to none. Evidently, best seller demand does not dictate the purchase of magazines for libraries as it seems to control the purchase of current popular fiction.

The libraries in the Inquiry sample, however, do subscribe to some of the magazines with largest circulations. They stock, on the average, 71 percent of all the general, women's, picture, news, and other magazines having circulations of more than a million. And they subscribe, on the average, to 49 percent of the popular magazines with circulations of 300,000 to a million. Here, again, selection on a basis other than size of circulation seems to be at work. General story magazines, such as *Liberty* and the *Cosmopolitan*, and the so-called snob and charm magazines, have much smaller percentages of library subscriptions than do the magazines of news, public affairs, popular science, and women's interests.

More striking, however, is the fact that the quality and opinion magazines, with circulations of only 50,000 to 300,000, show as high a percentage of subscribers in our sample as do the mass magazines. Especially is this true with regard to larger libraries. For libraries with budgets of $250,000 and more an average of 98 percent of subscriptions to these quality magazines is reported. But the percentage remains high in the smaller libraries until the $5,000 budget level is reached, where the percentage drops abruptly to 15 percent. The percentage for all the libraries is 68.

Equally striking is the large percentage of libraries subscribing to some of the fifty specialized, professional, and hobby magazines listed in a questionnaire submitted to the public libraries constituting our sample. The libraries with budgets of over $250,000 averaged subscriptions to 92 percent on this list. The percentage decreased to an average of 28 percent for libraries with budgets of $10,000–$25,000 and to 5 percent for libraries with less than a $10,000 budget.

With regard to the binding of periodicals there is a similar disparity between large and smaller libraries. In the very largest metropolitan libraries the average bindery list is 1,677. In smaller city libraries, with budgets from $25,000–$100,000, the average number of periodicals bound is fifty; in the libraries from $10,000–$25,000 the average is fifteen, and below that size, one or more.

It is evident from this sampling that prevailing public library policy in selecting magazines for purchase has some relation to large circulations but also is related to the special function of the library as an agency to preserve magazines useful for later reference purposes.

Such a policy is more clearly evident in subscriptions to newspapers. Many libraries provide reading rooms for those who wish to read the day's newspapers. But the tendency is to assume that the commercial distribution of newspapers provides adequately for current reading and that the public library's most useful function is the preservation of the back files of local and one or more metropolitan newspapers for reference and historical use.

GOVERNMENT PUBLICATIONS   A fourth category of materials in public libraries consists of the documents and other publications issued by Federal, state, and local governments, as well as by the increasing number of international agencies. The total volume of these publications looms large in bulk, the annual output of the Federal Government alone numbering more than 25,000 listed items. In most cases the documents are furnished at no cost or at very low prices. For public libraries the cost of purchasing government publications is, therefore, not a deterrent to acquiring them. The problem is rather to determine which ones to order from the vast mass of published material which governments issue and publicize only by including them in long lists of documents. The lists are not especially convenient guides to the library purchaser in selecting titles needed for his collection, and the government publishers usually leave to him the whole task of apprizing the library's public of the existence and value of the publications after they are acquired.

It happens that sizable public document collections have been concentrated in the 2 percent of public libraries in cities with more than a 100,000 population. The tendency is accentuated by the long-standing arrangement by which approximately 500 libraries, including university, state, and municipal institutions, are officially designated as depositories to receive without charge all or selected portions of the federal documentary output. Of the depositories, 162 are public libraries, including all the big city libraries and a few libraries in cities of medium size.

The large proportion of all government publications are valuable mainly as reference material. And they are handled as such in public libraries by documents specialists, with special classifications and shelving, rather than as materials to be included as constituent parts of the regular book stock for both circulation and reference.

Among the huge mass of official publications, however, are many books, booklets, and pamphlets which are intended for popular use and would form a valuable part of the stock of materials for general circulation and ready reference in public libraries of all sizes. For instance, among the federal documents are listed twenty-six "best sellers." These are for the most part how-to-do-it publications, of great value because of their simple presentation of important information of an authoritative character. Their total sales run into millions. Yet they are not stocked by all public libraries. We found them represented in the holdings of public libraries of various sizes in the Inquiry sample in about the same proportions as were the critics' choices of current nonfiction rather than their holdings of commercial best-seller nonfiction. The large city libraries with populations and budgets over $100,000 held, on the average, 80 to 95 percent of them; libraries in cities of 50,000–100,000, on the average, held about half of the twenty-six titles; libraries in cities of 25,000–50,000 about a quarter of them; and libraries in smaller places a fifth or less. It is not small book budgets which prevent the smaller places from including this valuable material among their resources. It is lack of skill or interest in locating them in the voluminous document lists, or the belief that once acquired they will not be used because no one will know about them.

These, then, are the traditional library materials: books, magazines, newspapers, government documents—all products of the typesetter and printing press. But in recent years some public libraries have been adding other and newer materials: mainly, picture prints, phonograph records, and films.

PRINT COLLECTIONS   One of the most unobtrusive and economical of these additional services is the maintenance of vertical files of prints of pictures of all sorts, classified conveniently by subject matter. The prints are largely clippings from back copies of unbound periodicals and other ephemera. These by-products of the library's current periodical service are often supplemented by the purchase of cheap print collections. But for the most part the only expense involved in maintaining the picture collection is the man power required to clip, file, and supervise the use of the files. The principal users of the collection are designers, illustrators, art teachers, and others engaged in commercial or applied art. For these people the print file is a highly valued resource. Since the art industries tend to concentrate in larger cities, most print collections are found in the large city libraries. But picture print collections are financially more practicable in smaller libraries than are most library materials and services, and they are occasionally found there. Print collections vary from a simple file drawer containing a few prints collected for a specific purpose to a large room with a battery of vertical files filled with thousands and thousands of accumulated prints. It is difficult, therefore, to obtain figures to indicate how widespread among public libraries this special service is.

MUSIC MATERIALS   In building a collection of reproductions of pictures the public library is still dealing with the products of the printing press. When it has acquired phonograph records and radio recordings, however, it has moved out of the world of print into another medium altogether. Yet music record collections illustrate how a newer material combined with books and other print (in this case music scores) may form a collection of which every part is more valuable because it is combined with the other parts. In a well-rounded library music collection the serious student can learn about the music of Mozart, for example, not only by reading about it in books but also by reading the scores of some of his compositions and hearing them played on records. Indeed, a library that limits its resources in the field of music to words written about music is not presenting music in its own language, which is that of notation and sound. The well-developed music division of a public library, consequently, has books of, as well as about, music, music periodicals, scores, and records and is supervised by a person having enough musical training and interest to relate these materials to each other and to the musical life and interests of the community.

In some ways the problem of building a library's music collection is easier than that of developing a collection of current and standard fiction. There is, of course, a huge public demand for ephemeral, popular sheet music and records, just as there is for ephemeral current fiction and nonfiction. But ephemeral materials are supplied adequately through commercial channels, even in small communities. In fact, there are more music and record retail stores in the country than there are bona fide bookstores. This fact is probably not so surprising when we realize that one out of four people in the United States now plays, or has played, a musical instrument, and that music in all its phases has become a billion dollar industry. The public library's field is clearly marked as that of serious music: classical, modern, preclassical, and folk. Its clientele, just as clearly, consists of the serious musical professionals and amateurs of the community. Estimates place the total number of these musically highly educated persons in the United States at a million. A most useful way to visualize a significant part of the public library's services may be to think of constellations of people, such as musicians, commercial artists, and other groups, that find in the public library the essential tools of their trade. Nowhere, except for limited groups in conservatories, some universities, and radio networks, are large collections of music materials available, unless they are made available by public libraries. And in our visits to library communities it seemed evident that the music divisions, especially when they were well directed, elicit enthusiastic response from and are heavily used by the music lovers and music practitioners in the community.

To develop a well-rounded musical collection requires more money than does a picture-print collection or some of the other library services, and it is outside the present financial resources of many smaller public libraries. Although the music books are no more expensive than a collection of books in any other special field, music scores require expert supervision, and a good collection is usually assembled only after several years of discriminating purchase. The same is true for a basic collection of 2,000–3,000 records, which requires several hundred dollars a year for new recordings and replacements. Of equal importance for a really effective service are staff members trained both in library techniques and in music so that they can co-operate intelligently with the musical leaders of the community in developing an effective library musical service.

The fact that a music division costs money is reflected in the limited number of public libraries which have been able to build adequate, well-rounded collections. Ruling out a shelf or alcove of books about music as not really a music collection, we found that among the public libraries in the Inquiry's sample adequate collections are concentrated pretty completely in cities of 100,000 or more. In this large city group, sixteen of the twenty-two included in the sample (73 percent) have substantial and well-rounded collections; three have large collections of books and scores, but no records; the other three have only a number of books on music as part of a general reference collection. There is a distinct superiority in extent and variety of the holdings of music material in the few library systems serving metropolitan areas which are also national centers of musical life, as compared with the other cities in the Type I group.

Of all the cities and towns in the sample having less than a 100,000 population, there are only four of the thirty-eight with even minimum collections of records and three with some music scores as well as books; the others have nothing that can be called a music collection or division in the sense that we have used the term. Of the eleven county libraries, only one has music records and scores in addition to books. The Inquiry sample of large libraries is not strictly representative of their whole number in the United States. Correcting the sample to eliminate public libraries included because of their reputation for extended services, the indication is that music divisions with books, records, and scores exist in two thirds to three fourths of the public libraries in cities with more than 100,000 population, in not over 10 percent of the towns and cities of 5,000–100,000, and almost none in the libraries in towns under 5,000. This means that in terms of numbers of libraries only about one in twenty-five public libraries, at most, has gone in for nonbook music materials.

FILMS IN THE LIBRARY   The documentary or informational film is the most recent nonprint material to be added by the public library. More than most innovations, this new library resource has been promoted by national library activity, notably by the American Library Association. Through its own officers, committees, and boards, and through active representation on interagency councils and committees of educational and film producing groups, the ALA has occupied a position of leadership in the movement during the last decade to build community machinery for the production, distribution, and exhibition of nontheatrical films.

During this period a number of larger city libraries have bought nonentertainment films to lend to community groups on a free or small-fee basis. In the last two years, with the active encouragement of a skilled ALA film adviser, the number of these library film collections has increased rapidly. At this writing there are about seventy-five such collections. In no sense, however, has film activity become a major function of the public library, rivaling its major preoccupation with books. In the most highly developed public library film centers the film unit uses a modest portion—2 to 3 percent—of the library's total budget. And the less than one hundred libraries that have gone in for films represent only about 1 percent of the public libraries of the country.

The limited development of film collections in libraries is undoubtedly due partly to the cost for even a minimum staff, equipment, and stock of films. But our studies indicate that the new medium involves a shift in thinking and practice on the part of many librarians before films will be welcomed as appropriate for library custodianship. Films require different equipment for storage and handling. They stem from a humble cultural milieu quite different from books, and even music records. Perhaps more important is the fact that informational as well as other films are designed to be shown to groups. For films the library patrons are clubs and societies of various kinds, rather than individual borrowers. Some public libraries do actually lend films to individuals when they are not in use by groups, but individual film use, if permitted at all, is a distinctly minor part of the library film service. Furthermore, the public library is only one of several educational agencies in the community engaged in purchasing, borrowing, and lending films. For these reasons a public library which offers films goes out into the community. It deals with organized groups and must build its place as part of a co-operative enterprise involving several agencies interested in films. Usually the public library film personnel serves usefully as members of a local film council or similar organization, with the special task of obtaining, storing, and distributing informational films and providing expert knowledge with regard to the content, purpose, and quality of the films it has acquired. Sometimes a public library becomes the home of the community's film council and co-operative film activities.

How many librarians will revise their thinking concerning the handling of films and how soon they will assume the responsibilities that go with the decision to include films as an appropriate service for libraries are still open questions. It might well be that within a decade practically all public libraries in cities over 75,000 or 100,000 will circulate information films. Extension of film service through public libraries to smaller communities, however, requires novel co-operative arrangements for circulation from a central pool of films to the small library units that do not own the films themselves. There are two experiments of this kind in operation now—a large city library film unit serving smaller libraries within its region and a state library film unit serving local libraries.

Two other public agencies are involved in film programs similar to those recently initiated by public libraries. School systems with adult education activities are developing information film libraries empowered to serve adult groups as well as schools, and university extension and adult education divisions in several of the states have created film libraries and rent films to adult groups within the state. Which of the three public agencies in the field, or what combination of them, will eventually be established as the film distribution center for adults in most communities it is impossible to predict. All that can now be reported is the present public library film activity, which consists of units fully and successfully established in a few city libraries, the beginnings of a regional film circulation network using a central library with smaller library outlets, a film information service rather than an information film service in a number of other public libraries, and active encouragement and promotion of library film service by officers, boards, and committees of the ALA.

LIBRARY MATERIALS, STRUCTURE, AND SERVICES   The account given here of the size and nature of library materials reflects both the characteristics of American public library structure and the prevalent concept of library services. Large city libraries are able to, and a majority do, supply themselves with books and other materials of great range and variety. They have current and bound periodicals covering a variety of special interests, prints, music records and scores, films, and government documents, as well as books, in the major fields of knowledge. Smaller public libraries—which means most existing public libraries—are unable in most cases to stock the newer non-book materials at all, and the smaller the library, the smaller the stock; but the smaller libraries also have a narrower range of books and bound periodicals. The result is that, except for the large city institutions, the community library is not equipped with the materials which enable it to provide the services defined by official public library objectives or implied in the assumption that in a democracy people should be provided with equal opportunities to learn.

Inability to meet the requirements set up by the official library objectives is not owing entirely to limited size and budgets. It is also a reflection of the ideas of those in charge of library policy, and these seem to vary with different types of material. Concerning the purchase and care of films, music records, scores, and prints most librarians see their function clearly as providing a service to people seeking serious materials. The holdings of these materials reflect that policy. Magazine holdings also show a tendency to select and to preserve periodicals which have a lasting value for serious workers rather than to compete in the commercial market for the patronage of readers of the current mass magazines.

But with regard to books the public library policy in many places is not clearly distinguished from commercial book distribution. There is a duplication of, in smaller libraries an emphasis on, current, ephemeral fiction and nonfiction. It is difficult to justify such an emphasis in terms of the official library objectives. Furthermore, in relation to government documents of a popular nature that represent the minimum of expense to acquire and fall well within the range of the library's announced function, many libraries do not stock them fully or systematically. Thus, the library's concept of its services as well as the limitations of size have determined present public library materials. The existing materials, in turn, inevitably affect the quality and amount of services which can be given.

6

LIBRARY SERVICES

It is traditional to assume that public library service consists of a general collection of books made freely available to individuals in the community who desire to use them. And it is still true that the most obvious picture of public library activity in America shows thousands of separate library units making available millions of books each year on all kinds of subjects to millions of people of all sorts, with wide varieties of reading and informational interests. To perform this function most libraries are organized into two major services: free circulation for limited periods and a reference collection for use within the library's walls. As we shall see below, the modern tendency in library organization is to distinguish particular subject fields and identifiable groups in the community as the basis for specialized services.

THE CIRCULATION SERVICE   Our studies and those of others tell little beyond a very few general facts about the service of circulation. We know that free lending is still the predominant function in most public libraries and that fiction comprises the major part of circulation. In public libraries as a whole fiction constitutes 60 to 65 percent of total circulation, ranging from 50 percent or a little less in the largest libraries to 75 percent in the smaller ones. In the large number of very small libraries, as we have seen, the book stock is most adequate in terms of current "best-seller" fiction and nonfiction. Existing studies, though not conclusive, indicate that the fiction portion of the library's collection has a heavier circulation than do other books and that the largest proportion of both the fiction and nonfiction circulated consists of current or recent publications.

In general we know also that children and young people, especially students, borrow public library books more than older people do; that younger adults use the library's circulation facilities more than older adults do; that the proportion of library borrowers rises sharply with their level of schooling; that women, especially housewives, are represented among the library borrowers considerably but not preponderantly more than men; that the same is true of white collar workers as contrasted with manual laborers; of single persons as compared with married people.

But as to what kinds of books are drawn out by these borrowers and for what particular purposes there are no reliable answers. The classifications of books and users that have been made lead only to the conclusion that the public library is an institution serving general and miscellaneous interests. The quality and amount of its circulation service, therefore, depend in considerable degree on the size, variety, and quality of its book stock.

LIBRARY RENTAL SHELVES   As has been noted in Chapter 5, small book stocks and purchasing funds tend to give the circulation service in very small libraries the special character of a lending library of current "best-seller" fiction and nonfiction. Whether the library is large or small, this part of its service shows a close similarity to the services rendered by commercial bookstores. A tacit acknowledgment of their equivalence is seen in the adoption by some public libraries of the commercial practice of daily rental fees for popular current books rather than the library's traditional system of free loans for limited periods. A rental collection for current fiction is maintained by half the libraries in the Inquiry sample. Only eight in the group of sixty included current nonfiction also on the rental shelves.

From the replies to our queries it seemed evident, however, that the librarians did not fully accept a position of being a direct competitor or substitute for the bookstore in distributing current fiction. There was indication that the rental system had been adopted reluctantly, that the rental charges were considered more as fines imposed in order to provide a maximum reader service for library patrons, like fines for overdue books, rather than as a principle for carrying on a circulation activity intended to be self-supporting. Without exception, the charges were less than those imposed by commercial lending libraries. In no case in our sample were the rental fees large enough, in fact, to maintain a self-supporting service of lending current, popular fiction or nonfiction. The librarian's attachment to the concept of free service may be seen also in the general practice of putting only duplicate copies on the rental shelves and retaining one copy in the regular collection for free loan. Thus, although many public libraries are carrying on a service which duplicates commercial book rental service, they insist upon distinguishing their service by lower rentals or free loans.

The special rental collections of public libraries have never played a major part in library activities. Their existence should not obscure the fact that libraries also assemble and circulate older and standard books of fiction and nonfiction, a service for which commercial agencies provide no competition.

REFERENCE SERVICE   The collection and distribution of standard and classic materials in public libraries merges into the public library's second traditional function—to serve as a center of information and reference. Books which have passed their peak of usefulness for circulation purposes are occasionally of some value in a reference collection. Having disappeared from bookstores and from most home collections they are preserved in the public library for later use by occasional curious seekers of knowledge. This is not to say that all the books, or a majority of them, bought for circulation need to be preserved for reference purposes or are useful as reference books—at least it would not be necessary in every library where they have been acquired. But reference material, though read less frequently than circulating material, has a quality of indispensability for the user which a single volume borrowed from current fiction does not possess.

Reference materials are not limited to books bought originally for circulation purposes. It is clear from our survey of the libraries in the Inquiry sample that even the smallest village library has some of the apparatus for serving the public as an elementary information or reference center: dictionaries, encyclopedias, maps, and indexes. Almost invariably, as the library grows in size, its reference materials and information function also grow. Aside from the paraphernalia of encyclopedias, atlases, and indexes acquired in order to answer questions, the well-stocked library will have comprehensive standard works in the major fields of the social sciences, history and biography, pure and applied science, literature, and philosophy. Thus, although reference and circulation materials overlap to a large degree and may be shelved in the same rooms, they serve somewhat different purposes and people.

To break down the reference function into defined, concrete services to identifiable persons is fully as difficult as similar attempts for the public library's circulation function. Even the gross numerical total of daily use of reference collections is unknown. This is because no regular record exists of the number of patrons who enter the library and without asking questions take material directly from the shelves and consult it inside the library. Our studies and studies of others tell only a few general facts about the nature of the recorded reference service. We know that actual staff work in connection with reference consists mainly in providing brief, simple answers to questions of all kinds. The studies show that two thirds to three fourths or more of the reference queries are answered within five minutes or less; another 20 percent within six to fifteen minutes; less than 5 percent require as much as half an hour to find the answers. Not only is circulation, therefore, numerically larger in the probable numbers of books used, but our measures of staff time devoted to reference work made in one large city library and two small ones indicate that it takes fewer man hours of staff time than are devoted to circulation activities. This relationship is probably generally true except for a few very large public libraries.

The fact is that despite the popularity among librarians of the concept of the public library as the community's center for reliable, useful information ever since it was persuasively enunciated by William S. Learned a quarter of a century ago,[1] the idea has not taken hold widely. Only a tiny minority in a national sample of the adult population interviewed for the Public Library Inquiry indicated that they would turn to the public library as a source of information on such subjects as nutrition, child care, or foreign countries. The survey revealed that for many people their library had little significance as a source of information. Their answers indicated that it just did not occur to them to go there for such purposes. "Never thought of it," "never used it," "too busy to go there," "too far away," "none available," "other sources more convenient" are typical reasons given for not patronizing their community library. Because of this widespread ignorance of its availability it is likely that the public library as a public reference service is an under-used institution.

[1]William S. Learned, *The American Public Library and the Diffusion of Knowledge*, New York, Harcourt, Brace & Co., 1924.

SPECIAL REFERENCE SERVICES   There are individuals and groups, however, in large and small communities that have learned to turn to the public library for special reference services. As in the case of circulation, the largest identifiable group using reference shelves and staff consists of school and college students; the bulk of their work is to fulfill academic assignments. Next in importance are adults seeking facts of all kinds, a larger proportion of men to women than in the library's circulation records. A staple reference service, however, found especially in middle-size and smaller communities, is furnishing reading lists and other help in planning the programs of women's clubs and mothers' groups. Many libraries have special collections on child care, with an expert in charge, used by both parents and teachers.

In the larger cities business enterprises and technical organizations have established close liaison with the public library. The public library, in turn, has built business and technology divisions under expert direction to collect, organize, and make quickly available background materials within the range of the specialized interests of the commercial and industrial enterprises in the community. The service includes continual alertness on the part of subject-matter experts to acquire valuable fugitive materials otherwise unavailable in any one place. At times the processing of the materials at the hands of the library specialists has become so complicated as to become a type of intensive research assistance rather than a means of quick general reference. As will be seen in Chapter 8, such specialized services have led to donation of funds to the library and recently to proposals for regular financial support of the specialized services by the corporations receiving them.

A similar special service for which the reward may come in larger library appropriations is a reference unit to aid municipal officials in their legislative and administrative tasks. Municipal reference divisions, attached to or detached from the public library, exist in many of the larger cities. They often perform work which may properly be called research. For the municipal library, as indeed for the county and state libraries, they offer a strategic opportunity to demonstrate the value of library service to the people most influential in providing the library's financial support, as well as providing a proper use of library skills for public purposes.

We have been discussing reference service as if it were performed by each public library as a self-contained unit. Actually it is not in libraries large enough to have professionally-trained reference personnel. By means of interlibrary loans and the photostating and microfilming of rare material, the community public library is able to extend its resources to include materials owned by larger libraries at a distance. The location of books and other material not locally available is aided by the preparation in large libraries of extensive bibliographies on special subjects, by union catalogues for a few regions, and for all libraries by the union catalogue at the Library of Congress. In at least one region there is now a pool of less-used library materials (state administrative documents, for instance) in a central library which can be called upon by any library member of the depository system. Here the initiative has been taken largely by university librarians, but the pooling device could logically be extended to include all the libraries of a region. The development of interlibrary loans and other co-operative arrangements is only in its beginning stages in practically all parts of the country. There is as yet nothing that can be called a network of related collections which makes the nation's library materials fully available to serious students in any part of it through the reference staff of his public library.

SERVICE TO CHILDREN AND YOUNG PEOPLE   Public library functions may be described, as we have done above, in terms

of materials (books, magazines, newspapers, government documents, phonograph records, scores, and films) and in terms of
the two major activities, circulation and reference, with a sub-
division of the latter to serve special groups. They may also
be thought of in terms of the two major divisions of the
library's clientele: adults (persons of working age and over)
and the child-youth groups (persons under working age).
Services to and resources for children and young people are
major activities of public libraries of all sizes. Juveniles, as our
studies show, borrow more than half the books which public
libraries circulate each year; a larger percentage of them than
of adults hold library registration cards and are regular library
users; students form the largest identifiable group making use
of library reference services; in county libraries most of the
local stations and bookmobile stopping places are public
schools. Even the smallest one-room public library is likely to
divide its shelving so that one side of the room is for children's
books and use, the other for adults. Larger libraries have children's departments, children's rooms, and specially trained
children's librarians. City systems have supervisors of children's work in branches and for co-operation with schools.
Closely connected usually with children's collections are
books for parents on child care and books on pedagogy for the
teachers of children. Recently there have emerged in a number of public libraries young people's rooms or alcoves with
young people's librarians in charge. These units, however,
tend to emphasize guidance in reading rather than a sharply
distinguished collection of books.

Altogether, public library service to children and young
people is an impressive achievement. In the last fifty years
library schools and libraries have developed children's librarians of great skill and personal effectiveness, with an expert
knowledge of children's literature. In many places they are in
advance of schoolteachers in the latter respect. Not only are

the children's librarians expert but also in the community they are recognized as such. Thus, children's rooms and children's librarians have been the classic success of the public library.

As long as elementary and high school work consisted of reading a succession of specific required texts, the public library had a free field in which to encourage and to serve the voluntary reading of a large and growing children's literature. In recent decades, however, in larger communities children's libraries have become one of two public library systems designed for the use of children. Rapidly in some places, slowly in others, but not at all in still others, the public school has been approaching the inclusion of guided voluntary reading of a wide variety of children's books as part of the school enterprise itself. Some schools have gone further, adding films, musical and other recordings, and picture prints as constituent parts of their equipment. There is even serious talk in some places of extending school supervision so as to include more pupil time by eliminating the unguided summer vacation.

As a consequence of this important innovation in teaching theory and practice, school libraries have appeared. In some places the public libraries have been invited into the public school to operate the school libraries as branches of the public library system. This practice has created a unified system of libraries for children in the community and has made full use of the reservoirs of experience possessed by children's librarians in building the school collections. But it has frequently created some serious administrative problems. It sets librarians, with longer hours of work and shorter vacations, in the midst of teaching personnel with shorter working hours and longer vacations, often with higher salary levels as well. It puts into a school service unit, which for effectiveness needs to be an integral part of curriculum planning and operations, a person whose primary allegiance administratively is to an organization outside school. Thus, frequently the price of a unified system seems to be friction and frustration.

A more complete formal unification of children's library service exists in some cities where the local board of education is legally constituted as the library board also and in others where the public library board is appointed by the board of education. In the places we observed, the schools and the public library operated much as if there were no such common overhead contact, so that actually no unification of school and children's library services was achieved.

The most common arrangement in our sample and in the country at large is the independent operation of the school library and the children's and young people's units of the public library, with varying degrees of voluntary co-operation. At one extreme we found communities where those in charge of the two units had never met each other, let alone discussed ways of co-operation. At the other end of the scale were cities where the school library and the public library systems operate as effective complements to each other in providing complete library service to the children and young people of the town. The school and public library supervisors meet regularly in joint session to select new books; there is a unified system of cataloguing for the two systems; an allocation of the pedagogical library and parents' collection is made to one or the other library system; the public library often provides temporary service to schools pending the building of school library collections in new quarters.

There seem to be no instances in which public school systems have broadened their concepts of school materials so as to include all children's literature, as well as audio-visual materials appropriate for children, keep the school library open and directly accessible for children and parents in the late afternoon, evening, and all summer, provide materials and guidance for preschool children and their parents, and in consequence have made it possible for the public library to retire from the children's library field. Although such a division of the library function between the two agencies on the basis of juvenile and adult groupings would seem logically to follow the completion of the school changes described above, there is no likelihood that such a radical transformation of school practice and scope will take place in the foreseeable future, at least not in the ten-year time frame set by the Inquiry as its limit for projecting trends.

In our discussions with school and public library officials in and outside our sample, certain overtones were apparent in the problems of relationship between the school library and public library. Among the public library group there was a generally defensive attitude regarding possible school absorption of the functions of juvenile library service. One deduced that the librarians felt vaguely that merely because of their much greater size, financial power, and pressure-group support the schools have an absorptive power. They feared that if the library function were taken over by the schools it would be neglected because it would become a sideshow in the total school operations, or if not neglected the school libraries would inevitably have an atmosphere of academic compulsion rather than the freedom and informality which now characterize children's and young people's rooms in public libraries. Much more concretely, it is realized that the public library personnel suffers from acute competition with the schools in salary scales, vacations, and retirement provisions, so that in some places an unplanned, irrational solution of the problem of the dual children's library system is arrived at because of the crude fact that in competition for the available personnel the school library positions are filled and the children's library positions are left vacant.

On the side of the school people, we found at least three recurring attitudes regarding the relationship between the two systems. Some had no desire to develop school libraries in any modern sense and were unconcerned or passive with regard to public library juvenile services. A second group, with or without any adequate libraries of their own, welcomed the public library as an asset and invited co-operation. This was especially true of some of the teachers and principals in rural schools where the public library provides much needed materials. A third group, small in number, yet influential in leadership because of their positions in large city schools and in colleges of education, feel that the modern school must control directly all its materials of instruction and that the materials must be greatly enriched so as to serve the general needs and interests of school children. They look forward to the school's becoming an educational community center open in the evening and throughout the year. To them it seems inevitable that school materials centers will gradually perform all or nearly all the functions now performed for children and young people in public libraries. They welcome public library co-operation, but they think of it as a transitional phase in the transfer of a function from one institution to another.

This, then, is the intellectual and emotional climate within which the present system of co-operative provision of library service to children and young people operates.

ADULT EDUCATION AND THE LIBRARY   Service to adults in public libraries is more difficult to define in terms of an identifiable clientele with needs for specific library materials than is any other type of library service. A library attached to a school, a college or university, or a business or governmental organization has a definite group of users who have specific activities to be served by library materials. The librarian knows what books, magazines, and other materials to order and which ones to duplicate. In serving adults the public library has no such institutional affiliations. It must be equipped to serve the potential, individual reading and information interests of the adult population of the whole community. The omnibus character of the service presents difficulties but also has great advantages. It is a service adaptable to various individual interests and needs. It serves a learning interest for adults which is free to proceed in any direction that variety and change of circumstance may dictate. By such service the public library is, in fact, an agency of adult education, the kind of education that has always gone on outside schools and will continue to form an important segment of the lifelong educational process. In some degree, in both circulation and reference departments, all public libraries perform this general adult service. Their competence in performing it depends directly on the quantity and quality of materials they possess or can readily secure for their clients and the skill of their staff members in marshaling the materials for their clients' use. In our sample we saw public libraries so small and poorly manned that general service to adults was severely circumscribed. We saw large libraries containing large book stocks, but with such poor organization and such inefficient staffs that general service was quite inadequate. We also saw large and medium-size libraries with such skilled staffs and organization that adults were served with materials of a range and quality which met the highest expectations. The size of the book stock and the quality of staff personnel seemed roughly to be the measures of adequacy for the general adult service.

Within the last generation, particularly, public library service to the adults who seek it as individuals has been supplemented by attempts to identify and serve organized adult groups. In this effort public libraries have shared in the widespread movement which has come to be called "adult education." Actually, organized educational activities designed for adults have a long and honorable lineage in the United States. And in greater or less degree mechanics institutes, lyceums, chautauquas, trade union schools, and agricultural extension services have had affiliations with community libraries. But beginning approximately at the end of the First World War there has been an accelerated effort, aided generously by grants from the Carnegie Corporation, to increase the extent and momentum of adult education enterprises of all kinds.

The early leaders in this movement were impressed by the great variety of groups, interests, and incentives involved in adult learning. Consequently they designed a loose framework of committees, a decentralization of initiative in organizing educational programs, and an omnibus association to include adult education projects of all types.

Public library activity for organized adult groups reflects this hospitable, decentralized concept. In our sample we found that most public libraries provide books and pamphlets, at times films and recordings, for special groups of various kinds in the community carrying on some kind of educational activity for their members and other people who can be interested in their special programs. Active, expert guidance in the selection of reading and other materials, sometimes in the framing of the programs themselves, is being given by libraries in many places to women's clubs, parent groups, and a miscellany of other societies and organizations. In some libraries, but by no means continuously in any one or generally in most communities, the public library organizes and carries on its own program of lectures, discussions, or concerts for adults. There are isolated instances in which the programs are centered in ideas, problems, or subjects rather than in books as such. The library books and other materials in these programs are merely instrumental in the same way that they are for school or college instruction. In most cases, however, the library-initiated program is designed for, or at least justified as, a means of encouraging the use of public library materials, whether books, films, or recordings. And it is active provision of materials for existing formal and informal groups in the community which constitutes the great bulk of the adult education activity of most public libraries at the present time. Obviously it is a useful service to the extent that the adult group activities themselves are useful. It has the advantage that the library can concentrate its collection and organization of materials upon specific areas which are of tangible service to identified groups. And it moves the claim for support of library service away from rather meaningless totals of registration and circulation toward concrete services whose value can be measured and appreciated in terms of the group activities served.

In recent years workers in the field of adult education have begun to feel that alongside the host of informal groups and projects carrying on adult education in American communities there is a desirable place for some more continuous, more professional direction and execution of significant phases of adult learning. At least four institutions with some claim to leadership in organizing this more formal, permanent activity were discernible in the states and communities we visited. One is the extension service of the state agricultural college in affiliation with the U. S. Agricultural Extension Service; the second is the adult education unit in state universities, municipal universities, and some privately endowed colleges and universities; third, the adult education division of city and state boards of education; fourth, the public library itself. In most of the places we visited the library is the least developed of the four. Agricultural extension has its own local network of agents for direct instruction and its own publications especially designed for its audience and available to them without charge. The colleges and universities have their own unrivaled intellectual resources and some centralized equipment for statewide communication through their own radio stations, film libraries, and agencies for books and other publications. The public school adult education activities have widely distributed buildings, equipment, libraries, and teaching staffs. The public libraries have primarily stocks of materials and staffs expert in knowledge of these materials, with some lecture rooms and classrooms, and only occasionally any staff member especially trained for instruction and class leadership. The present balance of human and financial resources, then, would seem strongly weighted on the side of the school and university agencies of adult education.

Naturally the question arises as to whether the public library, with its special skill and resources centered in books and other materials, should not be called upon to serve the other formal adult education agencies as it now serves the various informal clubs and groups in the community. Only rarely did we find a public library that is recognized as the library of these enterprises in the sense that school, college, or university libraries serve their parent institutions in the instruction of children and young people. There were instances of co-operation between county libraries and county agricultural extension agencies, but not enough so that the county library serves as the materials center for the extension program. In some cases the city school adult classes leaned heavily on public libraries for class reading materials. The same was true of university adult education classes. But in no place in our sample is the public library clearly recognized as the official library unit for the school, university, or community adult education program.[2]

The public library, then, has not become either a major center of formally organized adult education under its own initiative, nor does it serve as the officially designated library

[2] Not in our sample, but quite evidently a pioneering activity in the formal recognition of the public library as a constituent element in a university adult education program, is the program carried on in Louisville, Kentucky, where the local university uses the public library buildings and materials for carrying on an extensive, city-wide program of formally organized adult education.

for the existing major agencies of formal adult education. Nevertheless, to the extent of its means, in terms of materials and skilled personnel, the libraries provide opportunity for many men and women individually or organized into informal groups to continue their education as adults. In this sense it furnishes the essential library service for the host of activities and efforts which have somewhat romantically been called the people's university.

LIBRARY SERVICES AND LIBRARY OBJECTIVES   A description of the services provided by public libraries is meaningless in terms of averages or norms of accomplishment for the libraries as a whole. A salient fact concerning library services in the United States is the wide difference in adequacy between libraries of different sizes. This same variation was seen in the preceding chapter with regard to library materials, and both services and materials reflect the more primary fact of a wide range in library size and budgets.

In our sample there were public libraries with rich collections of materials which were capable of meeting the most varied demands for general circulation and reference; they possessed staffs capable of marshaling their materials for the service of users and, if necessary, augmenting them by loans from other libraries. In addition to general services to individual readers and students, these libraries, with varying emphasis suited to their communities, have developed specialized services to specific groups similar to those rendered by university and private special libraries to their clientele. Without becoming general agencies of organized adult education, they stimulate, guide, and even initiate such educational and cultural activities in their communities, furnishing the materials and the essential skilled service for these activities. Similarly, they co-operate with the public and private schools by providing rich materials of enlightenment and recreation, and expert guidance in their use, for the children and young people of the community. Altogether, the services in the best of the large city libraries achieve a close approximation to the official objectives which librarians have set for themselves and which are not performed by other agencies of modern communication.

But the public libraries with highly developed services are located almost invariably in large (Type I) and middle-size (Type II) cities and counties. In most smaller places the public library provides a limited general circulation and reference service only, without having the materials or the skilled personnel to meet minimum requirements of service as defined by the official library objectives.

7

LIBRARY GOVERNMENT
AND POLITICS

THE PUBLIC LIBRARY in the United States is today primarily a local institution. As such it is characterized by a wide variety of formal governmental patterns. The legal warrant for libraries, it is true, stems from the state. A few states have constitutional provisions, statutes, or court decisions declaring the library function to be part of the state's educational responsibility. But as we have seen, except for lending books by mail from a central book collection in the capital, state governments do not provide direct library service to the public even for localities which fail to do so. No municipality or county is required to perform the service. The initiative for instituting and maintaining a library, plans for its detailed organization, financial support, and management are matters for local action and authority.

In some states the legislative authority has provided a general governing pattern for public libraries that are created through local initiative. In other states having constitutional home-rule provisions, there is usually a limited set of alternatives for library government for municipalities that do not elect to frame their own home-rule charters. But this results in at least forty-eight general patterns plus the hundreds of special charters granted to cities by legislatures or framed by cities and towns under home-rule authority. On the surface, then, the picture shows great variety of legal framework for the American public library.

THE BOARD AND EXECUTIVE PATTERN   Despite this variety of legal form, the actual top governments for public libraries of various sizes and under separate jurisdiction possess considerable uniformity. There is prevalent the familiar pattern of an appointed board of laymen with legal power to manage the institution and an executive in immediate charge of its operation, appointed by and responsible to the board. This common structure stems from the semi-public associations, proprietary, and subscription libraries which preceded the tax-supported institutions in America. These libraries, in turn, derived their governing pattern from the basic corporate form of organization which has come to prevail in private business and nonprofit enterprises of all sorts. The board and executive structure appears in governmental institutions other than the public library at all levels. In government, however, it is less common now than it was forty or more years ago, before the movement for administrative simplification which substituted for boards the hierarchical system by which a single head, directly subordinate to the chief executive, is appointed for each public service. Public libraries, along with public schools and a few other public services, resisted the change and most are administered under the board form of organization.

The library board is usually of committee size. The range in size, in our sample, was from three to twenty-five members. The median number was seven, most boards having from five to nine members. The board members are local citizens, appointed generally by the mayor and confirmed by the local legislative body, or by the commission or council in cities and counties where general executive and legislative powers are combined in such a group. The terms of office of library board members in our sample varied from two years to life, with five years as the median. In order to guarantee some continuity in board deliberations, the terms are usually staggered. In almost all cases service on the board is without pay.

The boards in our sample possessed a large degree of autonomous authority within the general municipal government. Funds for library operations usually had to be obtained periodically by vote of the general governing body. In many cases the board was under some regulation by the general municipal officers in charge of personnel, accounting, and purchases. But within these limitations the boards enjoyed a broad authority to operate the library system. Actually, in all but the very small places we found that the board delegated executive management of the library to a professional librarian appointed by them for an indefinite period. But this delegation in almost all respects is a matter of custom and practical necessity rather than legal prescription.

DEVIATIONS FROM THE PATTERN   This is the normal picture of the top structure of public libraries. In our sample we encountered and examined a number of deviations from it. And outside our sample we encountered still others. We found self-perpetuating boards, elected boards, boards appointed by the school board, school boards serving as the library board, *ex-officio* boards, *ex-officio* board members, very small and very large boards with long or short terms, and libraries with no boards at all. We examined the deviations from the normal pattern in order to identify the structural elements which tend to improve library policy and direction. The quest yielded negative results. We were led to conclude that differences in board traditions, in quality of board membership, and in the librarian's professional stature and ability for effective top direction are of greater importance than any single element in the board's legal structure.

We found boards with long legal terms of office which actually had a high turnover in membership; boards with short legal terms, but a record of overlong actual tenure; annually appointed board chairmen who had served through automatic re-election for many years until they had reached their seventieth or eightieth year. We even found that capable librarians in a healthy civic environment without any board at all apparently operated more successful libraries than less able librarians with library boards. Evidently the important aspects of public library government are to be discovered, not in the legal or formal structure, but in the way in which the librarian, the board members, the officers of the general government, and the interested citizen groups play their various roles in the political or governing process.

THE ROLES OF THE BOARD AND THE LIBRARIAN   In defining the roles of the board and the librarian we again encountered variation on the surface with an essential similarity underneath. The variation, however, concerned the ways in which the roles are actually played in different library communities; the basic similarity is apparent in the concepts of the roles to be played. From talks with librarians and their boards, from the library literature, and also from the literature and direct observation of board and executive relationships in other social institutions we can construct a picture of the practice likely to yield the best results.

The chief librarian, as the leader of the professional staff, should be responsible for execution of policy in accordance with professional knowledge and skill. In the role of chief executive the librarian should also be responsible for proposing and interpreting the public library's program before the board, before the general legislative and appropriating bodies, and before the community at large. In this role he should contrive as far as possible to contribute to the board's understanding of policy so that its adoption by the board will be accompanied by conviction and willing sponsorship.

Policy determination, however, should be a shared function. It should represent the interaction of the librarian's expert knowledge with the common sense of the board's lay point of view, checked by the community patterns of thinking.

The board's share in adopting policy is important. Its chief function, however, should be sponsorship of the library's program before the municipal governing authority and the community. Librarians, in times past, have described this mediating activity as a buffer against political control of the library. But nowadays the board's sponsoring function is seen more positively as a means of effective access to the community's political authority and the appropriating power.

Willing sponsorship is not easily achieved. It results from the board's continued confidence in the librarian. To base confidence on knowledge implies responsibility for evaluating the librarian's performance. This requires access, on occasion, to the expert judgments of other professional librarians regarding the local librarian's competence as well as some contact with library staff members and library users.

Board members frequently perform less critical functions, not as laymen, but as experts in special skills needed for library planning and operation, but not needed often enough to justify appointment of a paid staff member to perform them. Thus, the lawyers on a board often furnish necessary legal counsel on library projects and problems, architects or builder members advise on problems of physical plant, banker members usually determine the investment of library funds and endowments. These are all important contributions to library administration. But lay policy judgments and sponsorship should remain the board's major services.

The foregoing description of the appropriate roles of the library board and the librarian in the political process is widely accepted as desirable. Actual performance, however, does not always follow this pattern. The relationships, as defined, are

sophisticated, calling for a librarian who sees the chief executive position as requiring political skill combined with administrative expertness and professional knowledge, and a board
characterized by good judgment, respect for expert librarianship, public spirit, and a prestige which extends to the major
power groups in the community.

BUDGET MAKING AND APPOINTMENTS   In order to get a
closer picture of the actual working relationships between the
chief librarians and library boards in our sample, we analyzed
three key political processes: making and adopting the library
budget, appointing the personnel, and book selection.

Discussion and review of the librarian's budget proposals
occupied an important place on the library board's agenda in
most of the sample libraries. But there were only a few in
which the librarian's persuasive power in the process of
budget review and adoption resulted in the board's taking up
the cudgels actively before the mayor, the council, and the
community for a program of enlarged expenditures for books
and salaries. In most places the librarian himself presented and
defended the budget before the mayor and the council. In too
many cases the library budget was a fixed amount from year to
year, so small in proportion to total municipal expenditure that
it was passed by the appropriating authorities without a
struggle, or was subjected to such horizontal percentage cuts as
were applied to all other public services. When there was need
for enlarged or new library buildings there was observable an
increase of participation by board members in the campaign
for funds.

Except for very small institutions where the librarian is still
a clerk rather than an executive, appointments to the library
staff in our sample were left pretty completely to the librarian's initiative and decision. The board was often consulted on
appointments to the chief positions under the librarian. Oc-

casionally board members interviewed candidates for such positions. But in most cases the board was content formally to review and approve the librarian's choices for staff members.

BOOK SELECTION AND CENSORSHIP   In all but the smallest public libraries in our sample, book selection was carried on principally by the librarian and his staff. We did find that most of the library boards had a committee on book selection. In many cases the committee is a survival from the old association libraries in which the governing board chose the books for the librarian to care for and to lend. But in our sample the book committees were among the least active. The work of selection was usually a routine process involving many members of the professional staff, and the choices were made on a professional basis.

Book selection, of course, in all but a few public libraries prosperous enough to purchase almost everything that is published, involves book rejection. This necessity of choosing from the huge mass of available material is shared by the library with all other large-scale agencies of general communication. But the public library's responsibility for avoiding censorship is greater than that of private agencies. The constitutional right of a free press in the United States is specifically the right of private persons to publish their ideas unhindered by governmental limitation. But as was indicated in Chapter 1, the broader assumption behind the legal right is that there is a long-time social advantage in maintaining the widest possible area of bold, diverse oral and printed expression and communication. At the same time, the assumption behind government activities is that they shall promote public order, morality, and decency. The public library, therefore, as part of the government, cannot escape the reponsibility either for careful selection on the basis of quality or for maintaining the widest possible area of free communication. It must reject, but it may not censor.

Here a clear understanding of terms may be helpful. A dictionary definition of censorship, "withholding from publication that which is objectionable," does not get us very far. An operational definition applied to libraries identifies censorship as the rejection by a library authority of a book (or other material) which the librarian, the library board, or some person (or persons) bringing pressure on them holds to be obscene, dangerously radical, subversive, or too critical of the existing mores. It distinguishes such action from the rejection of a book on the ground that it is of little worth as fact, idea, or literature, is too expensive, duplicates existing holdings, or is undesirable on some other practical ground. The line between this professional act of rejection and the political act of censorship cannot be sharply drawn. The public library, therefore, in selecting books is carrying on a discretionary function which may be a matter of public policy.

Experience in the various libraries we visited illustrates this fact. There were reported instances of attempts by minorities to exercise pressure against the purchase of books for the library which justly or unjustly attacked the minority's cherished institutions or practices. There were cases in which local economic groups resented the library's acquisition of books which criticize the economic *status quo*. On the other side, there were reports of protests by leftist groups against the purchase of writings in defense of the *status quo* or attacking communism. In some communities, the library was denounced by professional vestal virgins for harboring books which discussed, honestly, or otherwise, the serious, modern problems of sex, adultery, divorce, and perversion. On the other hand, librarians were importuned by cultist groups to display tracts parading their fanatical views. There were also reported pressures from those who thought that the public library's posses-

sion of books by Russian communists about Russia meant that
the librarian was a communist rather than a patriotic citizen
attempting to further an understanding of the mentality and
the aims of one of the two great powers in the contemporary
world.

In answer to our direct questions, the librarians in our
sample, almost without exception, expressed approval of the
inclusion of material on all sides of public questions and the
maintenance of the broadest possible basis of book selection.
Only a minority stated that the pressures on them from the
board members or groups in the community were frequent or
important, and even fewer reported pressures that had resulted
in actual censorship of the questioned books. There was considerable spread of opinion among the librarians as to the
proper course of action in the face of a library board's instruction to exercise censorship in purchases. Some felt that since
the board represents the popular will, the librarian was fully
justified in following the board's instruction as part of the
democratic process. Others, however, felt that the librarian
had a professional responsibility to resist censorship pressures
from either board members or citizen groups. We encountered
instances in which the librarian had exercised both courage
and political skill in revealing the pressures as those of minorities rather than majorities and in resisting them successfully.

It is worth noting that among all the media of modern public communication the public library is technically best suited
to be a chief citadel of free communication. Unlike newspapers, radio, movies, magazines, and television, libraries do
not wrap material of all kinds for all ages in one bundle for de-
livery in the home. People must seek out separate items in libraries. Material held to be unsuitable for children can readily
be kept off shelves to which children have direct access. Even
books for adults, such as some medical literature which librarians believe should not be available to all and sundry, can and

are shelved in the librarian's office to be lent to qualified persons on their application only.

Whether because of this favorable position for free communication, because of a professional ethic inculcated in library schools and library literature, or for other reasons, it was obvious to us that the official climate of librarians tends to be liberal. At least this was true of opinion expressed to us as outside Inquirers. Of the actual practice of selection in relation to books subject elsewhere to pressures or censorship, we were able to get only small samplings.

In 1948, 79 percent of the libraries in our sample purchased Alfred Kinsey's *Sexual Behavior in the Human Male* as compared with an average of 85 percent that purchased the year's list of other nonfiction best sellers. It was bought, often with several duplicate copies, by every library in the sample having a budget of $25,000 or more, by 80 percent of the libraries with budgets of $10,000–$25,000, but by only one of the nine libraries having budgets under $10,000. The Kinsey book was relatively expensive. Whether the smaller libraries, with severely limited book budgets, failed to buy it because of its cost or because of its contents it is impossible to say.

The record is clearer in the case of two novels on the 1948 list of "notable books" chosen by a committee of the American Library Association. Lockridge's *Raintree County* was declared obscene by the courts in one state; Mailer's *The Naked and the Dead* was criticized in some quarters for too great frankness in dealing with sex matters. *Raintree County* was purchased, singly or with duplicates, by 97 percent (all but two libraries—one in a large city, the other in a small town) of the public libraries in our sample; it and one other book were listed as having been purchased by the largest number of libraries. The Mailer novel was bought by 94 percent of our libraries, a higher proportion than the average of 88 percent for the whole list of "notable fiction."

These samplings of 1948 book selections by widely-distributed public libraries of all sizes indicate that to some extent library practices bear a real relation to the professions of librarians in the matter of censorship.[1]

We were able to get a somewhat impressionistic picture of the pressures on the librarian and his response to them by inspecting on private-office shelves the books which had been removed from the library's open shelves, but not from the library. These under-the-counter collections were in most cases a mixture showing both proper sequestration and prudent compromise, if not defeat, in the face of board or community pressures. In some cases the shelves contained relics of past bigotries long since forgotten. On the other hand, in a number of the libraries we found on open shelves volumes presenting the unpopular view on highly controversial subjects in those particular communities.

The evidence available to us did not lead to any reliable conclusions regarding book selection in relation to censorship in American public libraries. Except in very small libraries where there is no professional librarian, the selections seemed to be made primarily by the librarian and the staff on a professional basis. Political intervention, direct or subtly suggested by board members or citizen groups, as well as the timidities of some librarians, had often resulted in a middle course between complete rejection of controversial titles and their display on open shelves. But there seemed to be little overt, ac-

[1] A recent study of the social attitudes of librarians and their emphasis in book purchases on social issues, in libraries serving cities of 20,000–50,000 population, found that the majority of librarians were middle-of-the-road in politico-social attitudes, that they were given a pretty free hand by library boards in book selection, that the majority adhered to belief in impartiality and balance in acquisition and promotion of books on social issues, and that the more "liberal" librarians purchased more titles than others dealing with social issues, but selected the titles with various points of view rather than with one bias only. See Clyde L. Haselden, The Social Attitudes of Librarians and the Selection of Books on Social Issues, University of Chicago, June, 1948. (Manuscript master's thesis.)

knowledged censorship and few cases of persistent, regular
exercise of successful pressures by outside persons or groups
on the librarian's selection of new books.

DEVIATIONS FROM RECOMMENDED PRACTICE   In matters
other than budget making, appointments, and book selection,
we found procedures with regard to personnel that deviated
from the roles assigned in accepted theory to the librarian and
the library board. There were small libraries where the librarian functioned as a hired clerk of the board and acted
merely as custodian of the library's books, the board, or board
chairman, carrying on the management functions. We found
boards whose meetings were cluttered with detailed motions
and legal approvals regarding minor appointments and expenditures which could more properly have been settled by the librarian. We found small boards no larger than a working
committee divided into even smaller committees that were performing functions that might better have been dealt with by
the whole board or by individual members on an *ad hoc* basis.
In only a few libraries did we find boards whose times of
meeting, agenda, and other arrangements were contrived by
the librarian and the board chairman so that deliberations were
centered on major policies and important problems.

Some library boards in our sample have members who
never step into the library except for board meetings; others
by too-frequent visits and nagging interfere with the proper
performance of professional tasks by professional personnel.
We found boards that had irresponsibly re-elected the same
chairman year after year long after he or she was able to
attend meetings, let alone exercise any considerable leadership.
Some of the boards were constituted so as to give representation automatically to the community's various religious,
nationalistic, and occupational groups. They were thus needless replicas of the city's legislative body, unfitted for broader

representation before the whole community of the public library as a general service. We found boards very narrowly
constituted so that their membership consisted of congenial
persons whose access to the major power groups in the community was severely limited. Frequently we found that the
board included a lawyer, a banker, a businessman, an architect
or building contractor, a school man, a clergyman, a house-
wife, and the woman's club leader. Seldom did we find a trade
union official, the farm group leader, an engineer-technician,
a college or university faculty member or officer, a business
woman, a public administrator, or an expert in political skills,
whose counsel is needed as surely and as often by the public
library as is legal and architectural counsel. We seldom found
that young people were members.

These deviations from recommended practice occurred
frequently enough to indicate their importance as limitations
on the effectiveness of present-day public library government.
In one aspect of the political process there were so few deviations from good practice as to suggest that public library
government is sound in this respect. These were the isolated
instances in which library board members, city politicians
or party officials working through board members, have
placed political workers, friends, or relatives in library jobs,
have misappropriated library funds, mishandled library in-
vestments for personal gain, or favored personal or political
friends in purchasing library supplies. Although such inroads
of the spoilsman and the political machine are not unknown
in public library history, they have occurred very rarely.
Clearly, the general atmosphere of library government is one
of personal and professional integrity. It forms a tradition of
honest public service of great value in stimulating self-respect
among the members of library staffs. It is also a factor in maintaining the confidence and quiet prestige which the surveys of
citizen attitudes conducted by us and other agencies show to

exist towards the community library. Unfortunately, as we shall later see, this good opinion does not carry with it spontaneous public generosity in the matter of public library appropriations.

The foregoing analysis of the working relationship between the professional executive head and the lay governing board, although limited to public libraries, is not peculiar to them. A survey of the functioning of boards and executives in hospitals, schools, colleges, and welfare agencies would reveal a catalogue of the same or similar deviations from good practice. The universality of defective relationships, however, does not justify dismissing them as necessary or inevitable. It remains for the public library to solve such problems if it is to obtain community support adequate for the vigorous pursuit of its official goals.

SPONSORING CITIZEN GROUPS   The librarian as executive leader, the library board as lay critic and sponsor, and the mayor and council as appropriating authorities do not play the only roles in the political process involved in modern public library government. True, in a number of communities we visited this limited view of leadership and sponsorship seemed to prevail. In such places the librarian accepted an almost static situation with regard to library services and expenditures. Consequently, with or without the board's help he was able to have his small budget approved year after year by the municipal appropriating body as a matter of routine and tradition with only a perfunctory showing of actual library use in terms of the number of registrants, books circulated, and books purchased.

The difficulty with such a comparatively effortless procedure is that a library with a fixed or static budget is a library in the process of degeneration. Buildings wear out and book stocks keep on growing. New services are needed and requested as library techniques advance. Salaries that were adequate to attract and keep able women on the staff when there were few other occupations open to them no longer suffice to recruit or maintain a staff of either women or men in competition with other positions now open. And especially during the period of our Inquiry the cost of books, of building maintenance, and of living were rising rapidly.

Public libraries, then, seeking to maintain or to improve their position have been forced into active competition with the other local public services for their equitable portion of the tax dollar. The impersonal records of individual registrations and circulation, reflecting the library's traditional services, are not adequate for this rough competition. Librarians know, as do finance officers and appropriating bodies, that such figures can be raised or lowered by administrative practices that have nothing to do with the real value of the public library's services to the community. Fortunately, as we have seen in Chapter 6, in recent years library services to identified groups in the community have been increased. They involve reference as well as circulation services and thus reflect the public library's unique function as a communications medium more completely than do circulation figures alone. The newer services to groups, clubs, and governmental and business agencies are justified primarily for their own sake. Organized groups, aware of direct benefits from the library, however, are willing promoters of its cause. Together they are potentially able to wield considerable political power.

Some public libraries, therefore, have sought out such user groups as allies in their efforts to obtain greater public support. Friends of the Library have been organized in many cities and there are a few statewide groups, usually to support a local building project or a state library extension program. Created in this way specifically to secure financial support, the groups observed in our sample tended to fall apart for lack of an incentive after their single objective had been accomplished.

Advisory committees, similar to the parent-teacher associations widely used in the support of public schools and organized so as to represent all groups of library users, were encountered in only a few public library systems. Such advisory associations furnish bona fide counsel to the library staff and board concerning library resources and services in relation to the interests and needs of each of the groups. Advisory committees, in large cities at least, thus perform a real function in administering the public library. But in addition their increased knowledge and satisfaction from participating in library affairs can be counted on to furnish incentives for urging upon public officials more adquate financial support for the library.

Activities of user or interest(ed) groups are properly called "pressure politics." Some librarians regard open advocacy of the library's interests and the exercise of pressure as unbecoming conduct from which the public library had better remain aloof. But mobilization of groups in order to provide a public service which benefits them has become an essential part of the political process in the democratic state.

THE LIBRARY PROFESSIONAL ASSOCIATIONS   Chief among the interest groups promoting public library development are the organized librarians themselves. As in the case of other technical public services manned by professionals, what the public library does, the initiative and drive for its improvement and expansion, is determined in the long run by the librarians rather than by the agents of the general government or by the public. This is not to deny the basic controls and continuing influence on policy and practice exercised by the official government and the electorate. But within the limits set by these agencies, professional librarians, like doctors, engineers, and architects in their fields, possess an actual autonomy. By controlling the selection and formal training of professional personnel, setting standards of library performance, and framing and promoting special projects and general programs, the American Library Association and regional, state, and local associations constitute an essential part of the government of American public libraries. These professional associations are also important parts of the political process which determine the place of the public library in competition with other public services. As such, library associations deserve special scrutiny.

Library associations operate in a structural framework and engage in political processes very similar to those of political governments themselves. In each organization there are the problems of (1) insuring popular control and general participation along with the maintenance of efficient central leadership and direction, (2) maintaining maximum autonomy for special, constituent groups with limited interests and at the same time insuring common support of a comprehensive program in the general professional interest, and (3) establishing a balanced relationship and division of functions between the various levels of librarian organization—local, state, regional, national, and international. These are, more briefly, the governmental problems of democracy, of horizontal organization, and of vertical organization. They are the persistent problems of any large profession of national scope whose members engage in various specialized activities. They are part and parcel of the history and the current deliberations of the American Library Association and the smaller groups constituting or affiliated with it.

Our study of the governing machinery and political processes of library associations led to the following conclusions concerning the ways in which each of the three major problems is being met.

ALA and, so far as we could discover, the regional, state, and local associations have created a formal machinery for elections, deliberation, and decision-making which follows democratic forms and procedures more completely than do most voluntary and professional groups that have come under our observation. Furthermore, the actual practice in carrying on the deliberations of the Association is characterized by a sensitivity to the democratic values of open discussion and wide representation which is very impressive. Like all large groups with a paid, permanent secretariat and with unpaid officers and committee members whose participation at conferences depends on time and adequate expense accounts provided by employing libraries, ALA tends to develop a group of insiders who carry a large part of the burden of planning, decision-making, and leadership. And from time to time this tendency develops a counter tendency among younger, ambitious, less conspicuous members to feel left out, neglected, or unrepresented. On two occasions, at least, in the last twenty years the ALA has experienced a successful insurrection of the outsiders against the insiders. Thus, although authority and influence here, as in other organizations, gravitate inevitably to the official leadership in most matters, deliberation and decision broaden out, on occasion, to include all those in the association with positive interest in a particular issue, and adequate machinery is available for making their opinions articulate.

One unusual device created by ALA to prevent a hardening of the arteries of intraprofessional communication is an audit of association policy, organization, and procedures by a special committee (called the Activities Committee) created periodically for that specific purpose. It reports its findings to the whole membership as well as to the governing council. The fourth of these committees finished its labors during the course of the Inquiry. Its final report, which included a comprehensive analysis of the three major governmental problems listed above, was made the subject of detailed discussions at library association meetings on state, regional, and national levels over the period of a year or more. In these and other ways it seemed to us that the machinery and practices of the library associations were definitely oriented towards democratic control and member participation.

In fact, the efforts to increase general participation contain possibilities of becoming self-defeating. Over the years ALA has built up an elaborate structure of boards, divisions, committees, commissions, and round tables which are successful in engaging the voluntary efforts of a large number of its members. But to obtain positive action, or even to understand what goes on in the jungle of 140 or more separate constituent units, often with overlapping jurisdictions, requires intimate knowledge of the Association business. The very complexity of the structure places decisions in the hands of the experienced insiders. Much of the complexity is inevitable in a professional association which attempts to gather into its orbit the varied library activities of the whole country. But a generation ago American cities and states began to learn the lesson that complicated structures decrease effective popular understanding and control, and they moved toward simplicity. It seems evident that the ALA has not yet fully learned this lesson. At least it has not developed simplicity of structure into a principle of organization as it has popular control and member participation.

One of the most highly valued functions of library associations at all levels, as indeed of other professional organizations, is the exchange of ideas concerning methods and improved practices between specialists in each of the several branches of library activity. A large part of the space in library journals and of the time of those attending conferenecs of librarians is taken up with this trading of technical experience among cataloguers, extension librarians, children's librarians, bibliographers, and other special groups. By itself serving as a clearinghouse for those engaged in similar technical jobs it is of personal, tangible value to individual librarians, a value which probably justifies its existence as the professional association of librarians.

But a professional association has another function of equal, if not such obvious, value. It is to organize and emphasize the concerns of the profession as a whole: problems of recruiting, training, salary levels, pensions, status, and programs of general library organization for the state and the nation. Only by such emphasis does the library association become more than a congeries of specialists or the librarians become active professional citizens as well as technicians.

A large part of the efforts of the officers of the library associations are devoted necessarily to maintaining a delicate balance between the centrifugal and the centripetal forces within their membership. Both the Third and Fourth Activities committees attempted to achieve such a balance. But they did not solve the problem. Probably it can be met only by a succession of pragmatic adjustments to changing situations. At present within the national field there is one large group, the special librarians, outside ALA entirely, and another group quite restive within the fold. No new organization or more complete autonomy is likely to solve the problem of professional unity. The need for unity is, however, obvious from the point of view of outsiders assessing the librarians' political potential on behalf of public library development.

The problem of relationship between national, regional, state, and local library organizations is also not subject to neat or final solutions. In the last quarter of a century the balance has been weighted heavily on the side of the national association. Aided by a generous endowment, ALA has been able to support and carry on a broad range of activities with a full-time professional staff. The large variety and wide range of its activities are due partly to the fact that, unlike the education, health, and welfare groups, the public libraries have had no national governmental agency to act as their center of information. In the thirties ALA attempted to have such an agency created. But the diminutive unit in the Office of Education resulting from its efforts has neither funds nor staff to assume a role which would relieve ALA of all its semi-governmental activities.

In the meantime the state library associations have not developed financial resources or staff commensurate with ALA. With almost no exception the officers of the state associations give part-time services without compensation; the list of officers rotates from year to year; there is no permanent secretariat or headquarters unless space and staff are provided by the state library extension agency. The regional associations operate on an even more marginal basis than do the state associations. In only three regions do they compete in vitality or member loyalty with their constituent state bodies.

In several professional associations having a geographical scope and purpose similar to those of the ALA, the national, regional, state, and local organizations are tied together by consolidated dues and a single membership. But the affiliation of the state associations with ALA consists only of representation of the state bodies on ALA's governing council. A recent proposal (by the Fourth Activities Committee) to unify membership met with considerable skepticism as to whether the result of such unification would increase rather than decrease the total membership of the professional organizations. Librarians are, for the most part, on low salary levels and cannot afford large association dues, nor can they attend frequently or travel long distances to meetings. There are no established standards of certification which can serve as a qualification for association membership and thus make it a badge of professional status. Librarians join the associations

because of the benefits in knowledge, the meeting of acquaint-
ances, and the sense of fraternity they expect to derive from
membership or from a desire to contribute to the profession's
program and strength. In some places the state associations
have recruited a larger proportion of librarians within their
jurisdiction than has ALA. In other states the reverse is true.
Many thought that to increase the financial burden of individual membership would strengthen neither the state associations nor ALA.

There are indications, however, that ALA is seeking in other
ways to build a strong underlying structure of state and
regional library associations. The direct use of its resources
and staff for this purpose would tend to create a balance in
the general structure of professional library associations. From
our analysis of existing library structures, materials, services,
and government, it would also seem to be placing existing resources and leadership at a strategic point for public library
development in the years immediately ahead.

THE POLITICAL PROCESS ON THE STATE LEVEL   Our studies
have indicated that library expansion cannot be achieved
entirely through the initiative of independent municipal or
county units. Nor would it seem likely that there will be a
voluntary confederation of the libraries in metropolitan centers
to provide a complete service to those areas. State participation in providing local library service, in some form, seems
necessary. A number of states, as we have seen, have initiated
programs involving grants of authority, of funds, of books,
and of skilled personnel—or of all four—to create and maintain
larger library units.

Some states have demonstrated the value and practicability
of larger units of library service by temporarily granting state
funds to one or more demonstration areas. ALA has proposed

that funds be granted by the Federal Government to finance library demonstrations under state auspices. But if Congress passes an appropriation bill for this purpose, its effectiveness will depend directly upon the efficiency of organized and professionally-manned state library agencies. Thus, the state agency remains the strategic center for public library development in the immediate future.

The decision as to which of the alternative governmental means shall be used to institute and to operate the larger units of library service will vary from state to state. Different geographical conditions, different structures of local government and stages of library development will dictate different administrative forms and financial programs. But the common problem faced in all the states is to persuade people within and outside political office that the inadequacies of independent, small library units are incurable except by state action. What must be overcome in all programs for larger units is a deep-seated parochialism which opposes adequate local units and services.

Political action on a larger stage than the local community is involved, action in which some of the chief participants may be different. As we have seen, the librarian, the library board, the officers of the municipal government, and the advisory citizen groups play the chief roles in determining public library policy and library support in local government. The state librarian as chief library executive, initiator, and interpreter of the library program has a role almost exactly analogous to that of the community librarian. Also, the governor and the state legislature are cast in almost the same roles as those of the city mayor and the council: that is, to weigh and balance the proposals, pressures, and interests of competing groups and to fit them into a total program which is both politically and financially feasible. In the states we visited, however, no state library boards were playing a part analogous to that of municipal boards. In a number of states administrative reorganization programs have done away with library boards altogether and have placed the state library agency under the state educational department or the governor. In others there is a small board, often entirely or largely ex officio. These boards meet infrequently and seldom have the time, interest, or prestige to serve as the effective sponsors of the library's program before the governor and the legislature as municipal boards at their best do before the local appropriating bodies.

There were a few instances of state Friends of the Library, but in only one or two cases was a library user group effectively organized into a government association for supporting a state program of library development. Admittedly, this would be a difficult task. The active local library trustees form the nucleus for such an organization. But a dynamic and influential membership probably must await the creation of effective user groups to advise municipal libraries.

The main burden of promotion of the programs of state public library development that we observed, has been carried by the librarians of the states themselves organized into state library associations. Financial and other aid applied to the rural areas only is not likely to gain either full librarian participation or legislative support from city constituencies. We found that only when the state's program was broad enough to enlist the full participation of large city, college, and university librarians and professional staffs as well as the town, village, and county librarians and library extension leaders has a significant result in actual legislation been attained. Furthermore, the building of a state library association adequate for its political task requires a paid staff and funds for office maintenance. It would seem, then, that the evident intention of ALA to use part of its resources and leadership to help strengthen the state library associations affiliated with it represents sound strategy for the development of public library service in the country generally.

LIBRARIANS IN THE POLITICAL PROCESS   Our review indicates the political weaknesses of the public library in the face of an evident need to develop public support for improved structures and extended services. The library board at its best can serve an important function in sponsoring the library program before municipal, county, or state government and the community. However, we found that often the board's personnel, leadership, and procedures did not contribute as well as they might to this end. Citizen groups which benefit from library services can serve the same function of sponsorship. But systematic development of these groups for the purpose has occurred in few localities and almost no representative state groups have been formed. As individual leaders of their boards and in their communities the librarians can do much to build library support. Many of those in our sample, however, were not especially well equipped to perform that role.

Librarians organized into professional associations are probably the principal means for library development in the country as a whole. The American Library Association has mobilized funds and leadership effectively for many library purposes during the last three decades. It has gone further than many professional associations, also, in encouraging membership control and participation and in providing autonomy for special groups. But it has not escaped the usual problems of large and complex organizations in securing and maintaining the loyalties and the interest of both special constituent groups and the membership at large. It faces continuing, probably perennial, problems in these areas.

The regional, state, and local library organizations do not have sufficient resources to enable them to perform the political tasks involved in state and local library expansion which are called for if the official objectives for public library service are to be attained. They have no permanent, paid leadership or secretariat. It would seem that it is on these levels that the political strength of a united and informed professional group would be most effective in improving public library service in the decade ahead.

8

LIBRARY FINANCIAL SUPPORT

THE QUALITY OF PUBLIC LIBRARY SERVICES depends upon the amount of financial support. Conversely, funds for libraries depend upon popular appreciation of the value of library services. Surveys of citizen opinion show that people like the public library as an institution; they think of it as a worthy community enterprise, although many who praise it do not themselves use it. The favorable attitude seems to imply respect for the community's library as a symbol and servant of culture, a function not fully measured by the number of users or the amount of use. In this respect it is like other public services, such as the courts, the police, and the fire department.

But, as suggested earlier, the quiet prestige of the public library has not of itself built up a large or influential group of citizens willing to do battle for larger salaries, larger book funds, and more adequate buildings. The fact that library user groups are in the minority handicaps them in the quest for funds. Of the regular users an even smaller minority would suffer immediately if the public library service in a city should be suspended, as contrasted with the large number directly dependent on the public schools, the water and electricity utilities, and waste disposal. Skill of a high order is therefore required to translate the realities of present library services and the potentialities of enlarged services into an effective demand for increased public library appropriations. In the previous chapter it was indicated that librarians have not regularly been selected and trained, or library boards constituted and their time used, with a view to mobilizing official and popular support for library development. Nor have the active users of public libraries and the professional librarians often been organized with active library sponsorship as direct objectives.

Yet it seems clear from our analysis that there is a wide gap between existing public library coverage, materials, personnel, and services and those which library leaders have defined as their objectives. Some of the changes needed to reduce the gap are changes of library governmental structure. But to extend and to expand existing services by the addition of new materials and activities and better-trained staffs costs money. Where is the money to come from? How much library budget expansion can be thought of as a practical objective in the decade ahead—a decade when national effort is likely to be concentrated on vast expenditures for military weapons and on economic aid to other countries?

THE LIBRARY'S FISCAL INSIGNIFICANCE   The first significant fact with regard to library expenditures is their relative insignificance. The current operating costs (1948–49) of the public libraries in the United States are just under a hundred million dollars a year. Although there has been an average annual increase of 15 percent in expenditures in the last four years, public library outlays have not grown in relation to all other public expenditures. The present total is less than one sixth of 1 percent of the public budget for operating the public services of all kinds. It is only a little more than 2 percent of the expenditures for the nation's public schools. Within municipalities, where libraries compete with other local services for their annual income, the best figures available indicate that an average of two cents of the municipal tax dollar goes toward public library support. This money outlay may be compared with nearly 25 cents going to the public schools and the average of 4 cents for municipal recreation activities supported by the government.

If we attempt to set the annual outlay for public libraries against total public and private expenditures in the United States for all purposes, the library item is too small to identify. Similarly, when we examine the national statistics of average personal expenditures for all purposes the amount paid for library support is submerged as a very small part of the money the average person pays out as taxes. Among items for which people choose to spend money in their leisure hours where elements of personal choice play a large part, billiards and bowling alleys, for example, receive about half again as much money as do public libraries.

The whole enterprise of publishing and distributing books, of which the public library may be thought of as a part, is not the major financial activity which its cultural importance might lead us to assume. It constitutes only about 10 to 12 percent of the annual expenditures of the printing industry. Current newspapers and periodicals, on the other hand, with which public libraries are concerned only to a minor extent, account for more than half the country's annual printing bill.

Furthermore, the government's provision of libraries as a means of enabling readers to have free access to books on loan for limited periods is not the only device employed to reduce the cost of printed communication to readers. The federal government's reduced mailing rates for periodical publications have as their announced purpose the widespread "dissemination of information of a public character, or publications devoted to literature, the sciences, arts or some special industry," an objective almost identical with that of public libraries. The annual subsidy in the form of these second-class mail rates was approximately $200,000,000 for the last fiscal year, twice the total currently expended for the country's public libraries.

An even more substantial reduction of the direct cost of publications to their readers is effected by paid advertising.

More than half the revenues of newspapers and mass magazines come from their advertising pages, less than half from subscriptions and newsstand purchases. These advertising contributions, made not by governments, but as incidents of commercial enterprise, total at least six times as much for magazines as is provided by the public for libraries in the United States, about ten times as much to reduce the reader cost of newspapers in cities, towns, and villages as is contributed in these same communities for their public libraries. The public library, therefore, is one of the lesser financial devices our society employs to reduce the direct cost of distributing ideas and information in printed form.

That the public library is fiscally insignificant in the national economy is, of course, not to say that it is culturally insignificant. There is no necessary relationship in the world of values between what is of most social importance and what costs the most money. The relatively small expenditure for the maintenance of the public library is due partly to the fact that it is a very economical social contrivance. It gives books a maximum use per volume, enabling every member in a community to have access to hundreds of thousands of books at an average cost per person equal to the price of a single volume if purchased privately. It is more economical than the alternative system of selling board-covered books to individuals and families.

The relatively low cost of library service probably explains to some extent the traditionally low temperature of library politics, since small, fixed amounts for the maintenance of libraries are voted annually without much question. This is an enviable political position so long as salaries and prices are adequate and there is no need of a program for library expansion, but as was pointed out in Chapter 7, it causes serious difficulty in a dynamic society such as ours.

A more positive aspect of the public library's comparatively small total cost is that a reasonable increase in the funds granted to libraries—even a doubling of the present total within a decade—would not disturb the national economy, strain tax resources, or even dislocate government budget structures. Increased military expenditures, adopting compulsory health insurance, or doubling the expenditures for public schools would present major fiscal problems as well as critical social decisions. Each one reaches down to the individual citizen to affect in important ways how he may spend his income. Doubling the country's expenditures for its public libraries, however, would cause almost no recognizable change in the individual's plan for his personal expenditures: one less movie a year for the family, a weekend at home, reading a library book perhaps, rather than an excursion on the clogged highways in the country, or a necktie less at Christmas time. In other words, the problem of public library expansion is primarily one of policy, improved organization, and political persuasion, not of large fiscal readjustments.

LIBRARY BUDGET ALLOCATIONS   For what purposes do librarians want more money? Their almost unanimous answer is, for larger staff salaries. Salaries are already the largest single item in the public library's budget, and in recent years the proportion of total library funds devoted to salaries has been growing. In 1942 the ALA found that the average distribution of public library expenditures was: staff salaries, 55 percent; books, periodicals, and binding, 25 percent; other expenditures, including wages of the maintenance staff, 20 percent. In 1944–45, however, the average proportion of total funds going to staff salaries for the country as a whole was 58.7 percent.[1] By 1947 the ALA, which had suggested the earlier dis-

[1] Actually, there is considerable variation in the proportions going to staff salaries and to the other major items as between individual libraries and between the averages for public libraries in different states. In 1944–45 the percentages of total expenditures for staff salaries, for example, were 44.4

tribution as a desirable norm, revised its suggested allocation by transferring 5 percent from books to salaries to make a 60–20–20 ratio. For larger cities, it suggested transferring another 2.5 percent each from books and "other expenditures" to make the proportion for salaries 65 percent.

The device of increasing staff salaries by reducing the amounts spent for books and maintenance has not represented any scientific reformulation of the best way to divide the public library's appropriation dollar. Rather, it has been an emergency adjustment to the postwar inflation of living costs and scarcity of professionally-trained personnel. It was probably a reflection also of the tendency for public libraries to operate within the limitations of established, static appropriation totals. As the costs for books and other maintenance were going up at the same time as the inflation of living costs which affected staff salaries, the long-term effect was likely to be deterioration of services.

Library leaders feel that the library staff salary problem has been chronic rather than the temporary result of inflation only, that the salaries of library workers are below those for comparable occupations. It is difficult to substantiate or to disprove this hypothesis. Nearly every occupational group, we may assume, has a lively sense of its own worth and feels that it deserves higher salary rewards than its members are currently receiving. But are the librarians an especially depressed group as regards the average and the range of their salaries? The figures available for comparison permit of only tentative conclusions.

SALARY COMPARISONS   A major difficulty is that we are not sure what we are talking about when we speak of librarians.

---

percent in Vermont, slightly under 50 percent in Delaware and North Dakota, 62.3 percent in Oklahoma, 63 percent in Michigan, 63.4 percent in California, and 66.3 percent in Nevada.

Disregarding maintenance and custodial workers, we know from the analysis of library positions that some tasks are professional, requiring the services of persons with a college and professional school education; others are routine and clerical and can be learned by high school graduates with secretarial or in-service training. Our detailed measurement of units of work in a small sample of public libraries led to the conclusion that only about a third of the library operations call for professional training and skill. This does not mean that the staff members in public libraries are divided into one third professional and two thirds nonprofessional. But in large and well-organized libraries they are likely to come within 10 percent of this ratio: that is, 40 percent professional. In libraries of medium size professionally trained staff members do a considerable part of the routine clerical tasks. In most of the small public libraries, people without full academic or professional training are doing both professional and clerical work. The educational histories of the librarians in the Public Library Inquiry's sample who were classified by the libraries as professional revealed that only 58 percent of them had earned the academic bachelor's degree, with or without professional training; only 40 percent had received in addition the professional library degree normally attained by a fifth year's work at a library school. Thus, less than half the librarians called professionals have professional training; less than three fifths are college graduates. An undetermined, but considerable, percentage of the time of professionally trained workers is spent in nonprofessional work.

Is librarianship, then, an occupation of a routine, clerical nature to be compared properly with other routine, clerical occupations? Or is it a profession requiring the four-years college education and an additional year of formal professional education, to be compared with other professions having similar intellectual requirements? Obviously, the average present "professional" librarian is something of both. Just what the proportion is in terms of nature of work or educational requirements is not ascertainable from existing public library statistics. Comparing present library staff salaries with salaries of other callings having equivalent training and work is thus a matter of crude approximations.

From the 1940 census figures and later estimates we can make a comparison of persons who called themselves librarians with the full-time workers in the labor force of the country. The median salaries for the two groups were close together. The only appreciable difference was in the upper range ($2,500 or more), where there was a smaller proportion of library workers than of workers in the general labor force.

The most relevant comparison is between librarians, school teachers, and social welfare workers. These occupational groups are manned predominantly by women and each requires collegiate and professional education. Census figures for 1940, limited to the women members of these professions, show the librarians with a median salary 8 percent lower than the teachers, and 15 percent lower than the social workers. It is impossible to know to what extent this comparison is between women in the three occupations holding strictly professional positions. Other comparisons of more recent years but either not so reliable, or not so inclusive, show the librarians' median salaries about equal to these two sister professions.

Whatever the exact situation at present, a 10 percent horizontal increase in professional library salaries would probably suffice to put them on a plane of comparative equality with the professional groups with which libraries are in direct competition in recruiting personnel.

A question of a different kind is whether library salary scales have been adjusted upward in the last ten years to keep pace with the war and postwar inflation. The inflation has

now halted, temporarily at least, with a cost of living index
at 167 percent of the figure for the immediate prewar period
(1938). A salary today, therefore, to be the equivalent in buying power of a salary in 1938 must be two thirds more than
it was then. In public libraries, as in other government services, the salary increases during the decade have lagged behind
those in most private employment. With the leveling off of
the inflation curve in the last two years, however, library salaries have continued to increase. The incomplete figures available indicate that with the current year they have, on the
average for the country as a whole, closed the gap between
buying power and money salary created by the inflation spiral.

This leaves out of account the effect of the sharp increases
of income taxes during the last ten years on the take-home
pay of persons such as librarians who are in the $2,000–
$10,000 brackets. This burden, however, is not one that can
be shifted from the librarians to other groups as a matter of
equity. Rather, it is a common additional burden of citizenship which must inevitably affect standards of living negatively.

THE LIBRARY SALARY LADDER   Adjustments of salaries upward to meet the competition of similar occupations, to meet
higher price levels and increased income taxes, go across the
board and involve considerable sums. One unfavorable characteristic of public library salary scales revealed by examination of the scales themselves, however, does not involve such
large amounts of money. The top salaries for library administrators compare favorably with equivalent positions in other
branches of the municipal services. And in some larger systems
there is a single assistant or associate librarian whose salary is
only $1,000 to $2,000 less than that of the chief. But from
that point on there is an abrupt drop to a salary level for
experienced and skilled staff members only $1,500, $2,000,

or $2,500 above the entering salaries for the junior positions. What this distorted scale means is that the middle administrators, department heads, and highly-trained specialists, have salary careers giving quite inadequate recognition to their skill and importance for the library as an operating institution. Unless these people can advance or transfer to one of the two chief positions—and under the law of statistical probability only a small proportion will do so—they have dead-end jobs financially. Readjustment upward of the salaries of middle administrators and experienced specialists so that the salary ladder is proportioned to the importance of the work performed would not require large increases in the total budget. To conform to the scales prevailing in other well-organized administrative hierarchies, the increases themselves are considerable: $2,000, $3,000, and in some cases $4,000. But the number of positions affected is small: four, six, eight, or ten in a sizable public library. It is estimated that the salary increases for this group would not add more than 10 percent to the whole salary budget of a library.

Such salary readjustments would affect public libraries at a strategic point. The Inquiry's study of personnel by questionnaires filled out by the librarians themselves pointed up the fact that there is a disproportionate number of men in the top public library positions, which further reduces the opportunities for advancement of the women who form the bulk of those in the middle administrative positions. And the questionnaires indicated that women in the middle positions constitute the point of lowest morale in professional library ranks.

SALARIES, MATERIALS, MAINTENANCE, AND THE BUDGET TOTAL
Putting together the estimates of obvious need for an increase of public library salaries, we have: an approximate 10 percent increase to assure a rough equality with similar occupations, and a 10 percent additional increase to create a more equitable

scale of salaries, especially for the middle administrative group. This is a total increase of 20 percent in the library salary expenditures, or about a 12 percent addition to the public library's general budget.

Salary increases are not the only financial needs expressed by librarians. Additional funds for books and other printed materials are called for. The computation of book needs, however, is bound up with possible savings following the creation of book pools made possible when larger units of service are instituted. Consequently, it is impossible to make any reliable estimate of the overall percentage increases of funds required to provide public libraries with adequate book and other print materials. A minimum 5 percent increase in the book, periodical, and binding items, however, would seem legitimate, to eliminate the reductions of that amount or more, noted above, which have been made in the last five years to provide funds for emergency salary increases.

In addition to printed materials, libraries desire to add films, music, and other recordings to their stocks. Public libraries which have included these audio-visual materials and have provided the staff to handle them report that only a very modest percentage increase in the total library budget has been required for them. The average is approximately 10 percent. This added to the 5 percent increase for printed materials makes a 15 percent minimum increase for library materials as a whole.

The third area marked out by librarians for increased expenditures is the extension of public libraries to the quarter of the population now without them. If we may assume costs per capita for areas now without library facilities equivalent to those for areas now served (although service to rural areas is likely to be more expensive than for settled, urban areas) plus the percentage increases outlined above for the served areas, library service to the areas unprovided for would add about 33 percent to the nation's public library expenditures.

Altogether, then, the estimates for the additional outlays given priority by public library leaders are: a 12 percent increase for salaries; a 15 percent increase for materials; a 33 percent increase for extension of library service to uncovered areas—a total of 50 percent of present expenditures added to the nation's public library bill.

The figures given here are rough estimates for the country as a whole. They represent no statistically accurate computation of exact costs for a specific public library program. They cannot be applied meaningfully to a single community or state without consideration of the present levels and extent of local library service. Many an imaginative librarian can readily estimate additional and improved services for his community which would cost 100, 150, or 200 percent more than his library's present total expenditures. And each item in his program may be fully justified as a sound social investment.

Our purpose in giving approximate totals of budget increases is to provide a concrete picture of the minimum amount of additional income required to close the gap between current public library expenditures and the needed expenditures already defined.

LOCAL LIBRARY REVENUES   If public library income is to be increased by half in the next decade to meet the needs defined by library leaders, additional sources of revenue will have to be found. Seven eighths of present public library income is received from taxes imposed by the local governing authorities. And the main reliance of local governments for revenue is upon the general or real property tax—in fact, a tax upon real estate. It is not necessary to discuss here at length the virtues and defects of this traditional form of local taxation. In an earlier economy, when real property was a main source of income and costs of local government were small in comparison with total wealth in real estate, the general property tax provided a stable, equitable, and adequately productive source of revenue. These virtues, along with the visibility of the property to be taxed and relative ease of collection, fixed it firmly as the basis for the support of local governmental services. But as property became widely diversified and the tasks assumed by local governments became more extensive and costly, the general property tax became discriminatory and onerous.

In the face of the new situation real property owners went to their state legislatures for relief. Instead of changing the form of local taxation so as to bear more equitably on all forms of wealth or income, most of the legislatures placed legal limits of various kinds on the total amounts which local governments might levy on real estate. In some states there is a percentage limit on assessed valuation of real estate for all local purposes. In others there are upper limits on real estate taxes for specific services, including a specific ceiling for libraries. The pattern is variegated. The tax limitations were enacted at different times in differing political climates and pressures. In some states cities are more severely limited than are the counties; in other states the opposite is true. In one state, Ohio, a tax on intangibles yielding generous revenues has been made available to school districts with the result that public libraries organized under school districts rather than under cities and towns have prospered. In some states the ceilings on libraries are more cramping than on other services; in other states libraries have more generous upper limits. Consequently, the tax limitations not only create a definite ceiling on the expansion of the public library and other local services; but also they are somewhat capricious in effect, bearing much more heavily on one or more public services in one place than another, for no very good reason. Because the public library is one of the smallest local public agencies, because it is not such a conspicuous and generally recognized necessity as several of the larger services and is usually not so widely supported through organized citizen pressure, it frequently fares badly in the competitive struggle for its share of the limited funds available.

Recently some of the larger cities have sought new sources of revenue as a way out of the financial strait jacket created by legal limits on the real estate tax. They have introduced sales taxes, payroll taxes, and other special levies, some of which bring in considerable revenue. But often they are difficult to collect in smaller areas and can hardly be thought of as furnishing permanent relief.

Other functions similar to the public library, whose services are local, but whose benefits are diffused and may with good logic be defended as general in nature, have sought relief from the static revenue situation by obtaining partial financial support from the state government or by transferring a portion of their activities to direct state administration. This has been done for public schools, public health, public welfare and assistance, public highways, and other functions. Rather belatedly, the public libraries have begun to travel the same road.

STATE FINANCIAL AID TO LIBRARIES   The amount of state financial participation in support of local public libraries varies considerably in different regions. In some, state aid is negligible or nonexistent; in others, it is beginning to assume fiscal significance. Pennsylvania and Ohio, for instance, contribute less than 1 percent of the income received by their libraries; California contributes nothing at all from state income to local libraries. In the nine states of the Southeast, where library extension has taken hold more than it has in most of the other sections of the country, a recent self-survey of libraries found that state appropriations constituted 7.6 percent of the total library income.[2] In 1944–45, the last year when complete figures were reported by the Office of Education, state aid constituted only 1.5 percent of public library income throughout the whole country. Even this small percentage was three times as large as that received six years earlier. By 1948, however, the total state extension appropriations reported by ALA, $2,171,000, were two and a quarter times the figure for 1944–45.

The mechanics of state aid to public libraries also varies considerably from state to state. The traditional method, noted in Chapter 4, is to make small money grants to local public libraries without regard to their size or quality of service. Such grants—$50–$100 per library in some states—represent a kind of token aid of no fiscal significance for the building of a modern local library. Furthermore, the grants have not been used to establish minimum standards of any importance. More recently, a number of states have used grants with the direct purpose of encouraging larger local units. The grants are in two forms: an establishment grant given to county or multi-county districts at the time when the larger units are formed, to help provide the initial stock of books and other equipment; and annual grants thereafter for partial payment of operating expenses. As a condition for receiving the state grant the local libraries often have to meet minimum standards for their personnel. In a few cases the state aid is based on a complicated formula designed to assist poorer areas economically without pauperizing them. The objective of the more recent systems of state grants is clearly to stimulate the development of larger public library units having a staff and a book stock adequate for modern library service.

[2]*The Libraries of the Southeast,* edited by Louis R. Wilson and Marion A. Milzewski, University of North Carolina, 1949.

We found in our sample at the time of our study no state system of financial aid to local libraries designed solely and without compromise to attain this objective.

At the legislative session just ended (March, 1950) New York State did adopt a consistent program of financial aid to stimulate the creation of county library units.[3] The state grants provided are: (1) establishment grants of $10,000 to each county library system; (2) annual grants of $5,000 to each county library system, and $5,000 to each county in a multi-county system; (3) grants to pay for half the cost of books, periodicals, and binding up to 15 cents per capita to libraries constituting the county or multi-county systems, and grants to pay for one quarter of the cost of books up to 7½ cents per capita for libraries which are part of a system providing central book purchase and processing. All the public libraries receiving grants are subject to minimum standards for personnel, materials, and services promulgated by the Commissioner of Education (in whose department the New York State library is located).

The existing system of small grants to all local libraries is retained as an alternative for public libraries which do not qualify for the much larger grants under the new law. The

[3]See "Report of the Governor's Committee on Library Aid" (mimeographed), issued Feb. 17, 1950 (25 pp.). It is not clear whether this proposal supersedes or includes the program for regional auxiliary library units supported by the state, now being tried on an experimental basis in one New York region. Indeed, the emphasis in the law on aid to county systems in a state where more than half the counties, at most, have populations large enough to support a library system of adequate size for modern library service raises a question as to whether multi-county units will be discouraged by the state's financial grants. The law, however, permits a grant to a county library system only when it serves at least 80 percent of its population, and the new regulations include as conditions for grants to a library system flat minimums for annual book purchase ($8,000) and for professional personnel (5). Together these conditions furnish some guarantee that state aid under the new law will not encourage the continuance of library units too small to perform modern library service.

definite change of policy in the use of state grants is stated in the following words:

The State has provided financial assistance to libraries for well over a century but the basis for payment of this assistance has not been reviewed or changed in more than fifty years. It now bears no relationship to the size of a library, the number of people served or the quality of service provided. Neither does it provide an adequate incentive to the improvement of library services in a given area or to their extension to areas now without service.

For the first year a state appropriation of $1,000,000 was made. When fully operative, however, the maximum state financial aid to local libraries under the various grants would be $3,653,000 a year, approximately 35 percent of the amount provided last year by local taxation for library support in New York State. This substantial increase in the state's relative contribution to public library service is probably its most significant aspect. It is also significant in applying aid on a proportionate basis to the whole state, including metropolitan cities as well as rural counties. The actual operation of the New York law will be of great interest to library leaders in other states.

We have actual experience with the use of state funds in much smaller amounts to carry on demonstrations of larger public library units. In Louisiana, for instance, funds and professional assistance are given to a parish (the equivalent of a county in other states) to enable it to organize and carry on a public library service for a stated period of years. After the period of demonstration is over, the parish unit must depend on local taxes for support. The record of continuation of parish library service under its own financial steam is good. The device of state demonstration, however, does not institute a pattern for permanent, combined state and local support of public libraries which in many states seems necessary to obtain adequate library income.

Such a pattern is provided in the few states that have set up public library districts or regions as described in Chapter 4. Here the state aid is in the form of books pooled for general use in one region, library staff specialists available to assist local librarians, and central book purchase and processing services for local libraries which elect to use them, rather than state money grants to county or other library units. The device of state auxiliary regional service units has the merit of fiscal simplicity in sharing the costs of library service between the state and the local appropriating bodies.

Whichever method is adopted by a state for creating and maintaining larger library units, the larger unit is itself a means of providing more library service for the expenditure of the same amount of tax money, whether contributed by the locality or by the state. The public library's unique service to a community is to make available the reliable, more permanently valuable books and other materials on a wide variety of subjects. But any one of the books in this category is likely to be used by fewer people in any population group than are the more ephemeral current best sellers. Only library units serving large populations with a large and varied stock of materials can justify the purchase of the more serious books on the basis of their probable use. Use of such a book by one person in two thousand over a five-year period in a public library system serving 100,000 people would wear the book out, thus abundantly justifying its purchase. In a library serving 5,000 people it would take a century to wear out the book by use, with the very unlikely possibility that it would remain valuable that long. A library system intending to provide a really complete modern service will include at least one copy of most of the trade books published during the year, a careful selection from the annual output of scientific and technical books, subscriptions to at least 150 to 200 periodicals of both the general and the specialized types, and a discriminating selection from the annual output of government publications. The purchases will include duplicates of the books most in demand. They will include, also, the purchase of a large proportion of the year's output of information and documentary films and enough new music recordings to maintain a minimum collection of 3,000–4,000 records.

As a minimum, the staff for such a modern public library service will include seven persons with professional training: a general executive, a specialist each for reference, circulation, acquisitions, technical processes, children's work, adult groups and audio-visual materials, plus at least ten clerical and technical assistants, and a transportation and maintenance staff of three persons or more.

The general maintenance expense of such a library system can only be estimated from present library budgets: about 20 percent of the total expenditures. In many cases a modern library system combining or federating several existing units will effect economies by part-time use for regional library service of specialists serving in one or more libraries of the combined system. A region also may contract for headquarters service and facilities with the large city library within its borders together with its specialized staff and services. We have noted earlier that contracts with urban libraries for extra-urban services in counties have not always successfully secured full value in services for the rural areas. But if county or regional libraries are supported partially by state grants, the state library agency can assure the state that as a condition of the state grant the urban library is performing the service contracted for.

Allowing for all possible economies, our estimates of the annual cost for salaries, materials, and maintenance of the public library service defined above, using present price and salary levels, would be at or near the $100,000 mark. When we examined the public libraries in our sample with regard to their collection of standard nonfiction books, their subscriptions and binding of periodicals valuable for reference, and their collections of music materials, films, or government publications, we found that the $100,000 budget figure approximates the dividing line between adequacy and inadequacy.

We arrived at a larger budget minimum also when we attempted to discover the units of maximum efficiency in technical processing. The Inquiry's study of processes indicated that a working crew of four persons is the smallest unit which can obtain a reasonably efficient division of labor between professional and clerical workers. Such a group can catalogue approximately 24,000 titles a year. This number of books can be purchased for about $50,000. A book budget of that amount usually means a total annual budget in excess of $100,000. There are corresponding economies in the processes of selecting, ordering, receiving, preparing for use, and rebinding books, pamphlets, documents, films, and records in larger units. Selecting books and documents for purchase, for instance, should require the same critical and time-consuming examination of the year's output whether 200 or 20,000 titles are actually purchased. Thus, the use of state funds to help establish and maintain larger units of library service not only increases the quantity and quality of the library services rendered, but also promises to provide more service for the expenditure of the same amount of tax money.

FEDERAL AID TO PUBLIC LIBRARIES   Despite the gain to taxpayers and to library users claimed for larger library units fostered by state aid, progress in this direction has been slow. As a means of accelerating the movement, library extension leaders have looked to the national government. They began to think of Federal aid to libraries at least thirty years ago, became officially committed to it in the 1930's, and since then have sponsored a series of definite proposals for Federal grants of funds to the states to be used for local library purposes. During the 1930's the proposals were attached to bills for Federal school aid in large amounts to be granted to state school systems. The library proposals themselves in these years were ambitious in size and shared in the philosophy behind the educational proposals: that Federal taxing power should be used to equalize funds available in the states and to rectify state inequalities due to differences in per capita income. But in the early 1940's, with the transfer of Federal spending to enormous outlays for military purposes (an impetus that still continues) and the failure of the educational groups to obtain passage of a bill for Federal aid, the postwar library leadership revised its plans.

A separate proposal of smaller sums—five to seven million a year in the 1950 bill—to be granted state libraries for demonstration projects in one or more state areas over a period of four or five years, has been introduced in Congress at each recent session. Thus, demonstration for limited periods, rather than permanent grants for equalization, has become the current program for Federal aid to public libraries.

The use of the Federal taxing power for stimulation rather than for substantial equalization on a permanent basis seems to be justified from a fiscal point of view. Our studies of variation in per capita income between counties in the same state and between the forty-eight states reveal that differences in income do not account for many of the existing variations between counties and states in amounts of actual public library support. Two other factors are equally significant and together carry more weight than per capita income in explaining the local, state, and regional differences in public library support. One is the average level of formal schooling attained by the population in an area. The studies reported in Chapters 3 and 6 show that children, young people in high school, and adults who have been through college or through high school only, are proportionately the greatest library users. Where schools are flourishing and have flourished, there public libraries tend to flourish.

The second factor that influences library support is urbanism. As we have seen in earlier chapters, public libraries in this country have developed largely as municipal institutions. The framework of public library organization and financial support has only lately been adapted to rural services, and as yet to only a small extent. It is not surprising, therefore, to find that the per capita financial support of public libraries tends to be high in states having a large proportion of urban dwellers; low in states with large rural populations.

These three factors influencing public library financial support interact upon each other to some extent. States with a low average per capita income have usually not built and maintained a high level of schools. In such states, because of economic circumstance, more children drop out of school at an earlier age and go to work. Thus low levels of both income and of formal schooling conspire to reduce the number of potential public library users. Also, though not without exception, states which have a large industrial and consequently large urban population tend to have a higher average per capita income.

Grants of Federal funds over a period of years to states with a comparatively low standing in per capita income, schooling, and urban population would undoubtedly cause more public libraries to appear. They may do a great deal to energize the state's whole public library program. But the major function of the grant is to stimulate rather than to equalize through use of Federal taxing power. Our studies show that any one of the states has enough taxable wealth to provide itself with an adequate public library service. As in the case of the municipal library's slice of the total municipal budget, state expenditures in aid of public libraries could be much larger than at present and still constitute a very small place in the state's budget. The present state library extension outlay is a little less than .02 percent of the state's total expenditures. If state public library aid were expanded so as to provide half of the present total public library revenues of the country ($50,000,000 of the $100,000,000 total) it would still be less than 1 percent of state disbursements for all purposes. State aid rather than large Federal grants for equalization purposes, therefore, would seem to be the major reliance for public library development in the decade ahead. And grants to the states to equalize and expand formal schooling as well as ingenuity within the states to create a successful operating framework for rural library service may be as important as Federal grants for libraries in promoting the demand for and the use of modern public library service.[4]

Federal aid for stimulation purposes under present conditions must be carefully designed if it is to achieve its purpose. Under our governmental system Federal grants to public libraries would be administered by the state library agencies. These agencies vary greatly in size, resources, and quality of professional personnel. They vary also in the extent to which they have developed mature plans and leadership for building adequate, modern library service units within the state. The estimate, from our survey, is that not more than half the present state library agencies are developed sufficiently to provide

[4]Our analysis of the comparative statistics of state library support revealed another factor probably explaining generous or niggardly public library support in some states. This is the existence or absence of restrictive tax ceilings bearing upon public libraries. We found states with high per capita income, high average of schooling, and a high degree of urbanization, with comparatively low levels of public library support. Other states with these favorable factors equally present had high levels of library income. In the former, severe tax limits exist. In the latter, the municipal tax limitations are not restrictive or, as in Ohio, alternative forms of local taxation have been opened up.

assurance that Federal grants would not be frittered away in activities yielding no permanent results. The library leaders promoting the current bills for Federal aid are fully aware of this situation. Their efforts are turned toward setting standards and allocating funds to be granted so that the state library agencies will be stimulated and improved in the process of demonstration. As was suggested in Chapter 7, the development of strong state library agencies has high priority in the program of public library development for the years immediately ahead.

FEDERAL AID TO REFERENCE AND RESEARCH LIBRARY SERVICES
There is one field which is indirectly important to all public libraries where Federal aid in substantial amounts would be logical from a fiscal point of view—that is, grants to the reference and research services of the few great libraries that carry the burden of accumulating and making readily available for general use the world's output of valuable printed materials. The institutions serving in this way as national organizers and reservoirs of reference materials include university libraries, a few municipal libraries, a small number of endowed research libraries, and some of the Federal libraries, notably the Library of Congress. Estimates of their whole number vary from six to sixty, depending on the standards employed for defining the resources of such institutions. Whether supported by local taxes, university endowments and tuition, or other local sources, the fact is that as centers of reference materials and bibliographical machinery these libraries provide a service which clearly overruns local and state boundaries. Each is a part of a potential national network of related institutions serving the scholarly, research, scientific, humanistic interests of the whole society. The Harvard University Library and the New York Public Library, for instance, are not serving a university or a city only. A day-to-day analysis of their opera-

tions would show widespread activities on behalf of libraries, scholars, and other serious inquirers from all parts of the country. The necessity of depending on local taxes or endowments handicaps them inevitably in their broader role and is an inequitable means of support. These essentially national services would be a proper charge, therefore, to be borne in part, at least, by the Federal Government.

But the great reference collections form as yet only a potential, not an actual, network. Each has grown up as an independent, unrelated library unit, with resulting duplication of acquisitions, cataloguing, and bibliographical work in many subject-matter fields. For a long time the larger libraries have engaged in *de facto* co-operation through interlibrary loans. The availability of quick, cheap reproduction of materials by means of photostat and microfilm has greatly increased this informal interlibrary service. In recent years, with the increasing volume and complexity of incoming library materials, appreciation of the need for interlibrary allocations, planning, and other co-operative devices has been growing. A few regional bibliographical centers and union catalogues and at least one regional storage center have appeared, and others have been discussed in professional groups. Recently, also, the major research and reference libraries have allocated among themselves the purchase of the total current publication in designated fields from a number of European countries.

There are emerging, then, the institutional resources and definite concepts of the machinery for a national network of reference, research, and bibliographical service. The actual allocations of purchases in special fields as well as the arrangements for bibliographical responsibilities, and other co-operative machinery, although much discussed in committees of librarians, are difficult to achieve by voluntary agreement. The specific use of Federal funds to aid co-operative research library services might do much to get the machinery into operation.

Selection of the libraries to receive Federal aid would undoubtedly present difficulties. In this task the experience in designating the depository libraries for Federal documents serves both as an example and a warning. Free deposit of government documents in a network of libraries outside Washington is a precedent indicating the national interest in the library function of preserving and making available valuable materials. But the unscientific method of selecting the depository libraries, on the basis of Congressional districts rather than on size and quality of the library's resources, is something to be avoided. The Library of Congress is very well equipped in special knowledge and standing to administer the actual grants after designations are made.

The organization of research library service was considered to be on the periphery of the Public Library Inquiry so that no special study of specific ways of organizing or supporting it was made. It was clear, however, from our observations and from the committee discussions and the writings of librarians, that a research materials network was considered advantageous to many more than the dozen or more public libraries likely to be designated for Federal grants. Advocates of the co-operative services see them as creating a librarian's library service. Through the smaller public library as intermediary the individual seeker for the unusual book or document not in the small library's stock would, they assert, be able to get what he needs from the research library center by loan or reproduction. More systematically than now, bibliographies on special subjects would be prepared in the great centers and supplied to the smaller libraries. Less used materials would be weeded out and, if not duplicated, would be placed in the regional storage centers without loss of permanent availability. By using the research library network smaller libraries would thus be able to provide indirect reference service to serious researchers for specialized materials at any point in the country where a public library exists. Whatever the merits of these claims, it would seem that in determining tax resources for library support, Federal funds might appropriately be employed for aid to the library reference, research, and bibliographical centers and services.

ENDOWMENTS AND GIFTS, FINES AND FEES   Up to this point we have assumed that public library income is derived entirely from taxes, whether local, state, or Federal. There are, however, two other regular sources of library revenue: gifts for direct expenditure or as contributions to endowment, and payments by library users in the form of fines, fees, and rentals. Together these sources provide about one tenth of the total income of the nation's public libraries. Endowments stem mostly from an earlier period before community libraries received tax money. Most of the institutions now deriving an appreciable part of their support from contributed funds are small libraries in the North and the East. In many of these village libraries gifts still provide more than half the total revenue. In very few, however, is the ratio of gifts to taxes for support of the library on the increase. In only about a dozen cities of more than 25,000 population did endowments and gifts constitute a major source of public library income in 1944–45 (when the latest comprehensive statistics on support from gifts were published). But within and outside our sample we encountered a few larger libraries whose boards and other active patrons were so favorably placed in the local economic and social hierarchy that they were able to tap a continuing stream of gifts. Especially noteworthy were sums obtained and used as venture capital to launch new and experimental public library services. Of more doubtful value were the endowments or gifts that furnished the major continuing support for all or a segment of the library's activities. In some cases funds which had been ample at the time they were given had become plainly insufficient for current needs. Often it seemed next to impossible to persuade the taxpayers to provide the extra support needed. Endowments and gifts are to be reckoned with as a means of augmenting public library revenues. But, on the basis of our study there seems little likelihood that they will expand so as to provide any considerable part of the 50 percent additional revenue suggested above as a minimum goal for the next ten years.

Fines and fees now provide a little more than 6 percent of public library revenues.[5] Charging fines for overdue books is an accepted public library operation considered necessary to insure equity between users of its books and to maintain a minimum custodianship over public materials. Fines, however, are primarily a mechanism of control, not of revenue. If they were to be increased in order to produce larger income, they would tend to defeat one of the public library's essential purposes—encouraging people to read books in their homes and making it as convenient as possible for them to do so. Revenue from fines, therefore, cannot be expected to contribute to the expansion of public library income in the years ahead.

As was noted in Chapter 6, libraries have justified rental fees for current best sellers, fiction and nonfiction, on the same ground as they justify fines: to provide maximum readership of their books. A distinction may be drawn, however, between these two kinds of fees. The public library rental shelf stocked with mysteries, formula romances, and ephemeral nonfiction is in direct competition with commercial bookstores and rental libraries. This rental service solely on the basis of demand, a demand created largely by commercial promotion, falls out-

---

[5] It is worth noting that in some communities money received from library fines goes into the general municipal treasury and is not credited to the public library account. In these places, therefore, there is no library income from fines, properly speaking.

side a strict interpretation of the public library's announced objectives. One logical fiscal policy, then, would be to limit current purchases to books judged to be of merit as sources of reliable information, important ideas and viewpoints, or good literature and to circulate them to borrowers without fee. The other logical fiscal policy would be for the library to engage fully in the provision of current fiction and nonfiction of whatever quality on the basis of public demand and to charge rental fees large enough to make the service fully self-supporting. In one case the public library would be saving an expenditure not fully covered by existing rental charges and eliminating a service difficult to justify as entitled to support from public funds. In the other case, it would maintain a popular auxiliary book service without any burden on the taxpayer. Either policy would represent a financial gain, although neither would be more than a minor contribution to the problem of obtaining additional resources for a 50 percent increase of expenditures.

We have been assuming here that public library users have the real alternative of getting current popular books from either a public library or a local commercial bookstore and rental library. This assumption, as our studies show, is true only for large and medium-size cities. Most smaller cities and towns and nearly all villages lack the economic basis for the successful maintenance of commercial book outlets. Most villages also, as we have seen, are too small to support a public library. But there are many more smaller places with public libraries than with bookstores. This fact may explain, in part, why a majority of the existing libraries in small towns and villages have a book stock adapted to fill the need supplied elsewhere by commercial bookstore rental collections rather than the books which the public library is uniquely able to supply.

The suggestion is made, therefore, in one of our staff reports that in small towns and villages where there is no bookstore the public library might serve as a general community book center or be physically united with a commercial agency to form a general book center. In such an institution, books, new or second hand, could be bought from stock, purchased on order, borrowed for a rental fee, or loaned free for limited periods, depending on the customer's preference, the volume of demand for single titles, and the nature and quality of the books themselves. The argument made for the proposal is that enlarging the library's function in this way would serve a primary objective for which public libraries were created: to make books available to people. It might enable people in small communities to have more access to more books and to provide access to books under the guidance of persons skilled in book knowledge.

Attractive as such a general book center may seem on paper, we did not discover any significant moves in its direction in either small or large communities.[6] The proposal runs contrary to settled practice in public libraries and the convictions of librarians in favor of a free book service. The suggestion is set down here as one possible way of meeting the problem of a community too small to support separately either a public library or a bookstore. It might become the occasion for a community experiment where conditions for it are favorable. This idea would not affect major library financial operations or needs during the decade ahead.

The third type of fee is described in Chapter 6, where specialized reference service rendered business and other institutions in the community has raised the question of special payments for the services received. Throughout the years reference services have been provided free of charge, as have all other library services. In a number of communities large in-

[6] In some instances small public libraries arrange to serve as a local outlet for a commercial lending library.

dustrial and commercial organizations have made such frequent, intensive use of the library's special reference facilities
that it has become customary for them to make annual or
occasional donations of funds to the library. Recently proposals have been discussed in the profession for replacing this
occasional support of specialized reference services by complete financial support of the particular service. It has been
proposed that contracts for the purpose be made between the
library and the interested organizations or that an autonomous
corporation be formed, closely connected with the library and
supported jointly by the organizations using it. Whether such
a service, half reference and half research, can be defined
sharply enough so as to be outside the library's regular operations, properly supported by taxation, and whether special
payments for specialized services will enhance or limit the
library's income and general services are questions for which
no answer has been found in the observation of public library
experience. It is not evident that library income is likely to be
increased to any considerable extent in this way.

Our review of present and potential sources of public library revenues indicates that the main reliance for expansion
of income in the years immediately ahead will be on state and
local taxation. It is possible that gifts may augment revenues,
and a rental policy may be inaugurated for current best sellers
which will add to income or reduce expenditures. Some additional revenue may be realized if a Federal library aid bill is
enacted. But none of these measures, nor all of them together,
can be counted upon for an appreciable part of the 50 percent
increase in income which libraries need as a minimum if the
institution is to realize its objectives.

PROJECTED TRENDS IN NATIONAL EXPENDITURE   A logical
need and logical possibilities for increasing public library income exist. A relevant question, however, is whether a sub-

stantial increase in revenue is likely to occur in the next ten years. One factor in determining its likelihood is the ability of the librarians, library boards, and their friends to mobilize effective persuasion to that end. We have examined this potential in the preceding chapter.

Two other factors which will help to assess the probability of increased library funds are the ability of the economy to provide the funds and the habits, preferences, and interests of consumers in spending increased income. The most reliable appraisals regarding both factors are to be found in a comprehensive and exhaustive study of the actual trends for income and expenditure in the recent past in the United States projected into the proximate future, 1941–60, which has recently been completed by the Twentieth Century Fund.[7] The analysis showed an expected increase in gross national production per capita from 1941 to 1960 of 34 percent, 17 percent from 1951 to 1960. This means that as far as total resources are concerned the public library can with reasonable safety count on the ability of the economy to support increased expenditures on a gradually ascending curve. If, however, the public library is to receive only a proportionate share of increased income from the expanding national income, its percentage of increase may be less than the 50 percent posited above on the basis of defined need.

Is the public library likely to receive more or less than a proportionate share of the general increase? The Twentieth Century Fund study indicates to what products and services the increases will go if present trends continue throughout the

[7] J. Frederic Dewhurst and associates, *America's Needs and Resources*, New York, The Twentieth Century Fund, 1947. The Twentieth Century Fund is now engaged in revising its estimates on the basis of the actual experience of the years since 1941. Preliminary figures indicate that the projections proved to be too conservative in many cases. Furthermore, the increase of price levels in the intervening years has resulted in larger percentage increases of dollar expenditures than were estimated originally.

next decade. The trend lines for public library expenditures from 1951 to 1960 indicate increases falling within a low expectation of 13 percent and a high expectation of 30 percent. Broadening its analysis by projecting the existing trends of both public and private expenditure, the study indicated where the bulk of the extra money is likely to go in the next ten years. Almost half the increase is expected to go into consumer expenditures. Among consumer expenditures some of the increases per capita expected for the period 1941–1960 are: for consumer transportation, 45 percent; for food, liquor, and tobacco, 22 percent; and for recreation, 36 percent. Within the category of recreation, the expected increase for reading is only 14 percent. Thus, according to present trends expenditures for reading as recreation will not increase so rapidly when incomes rise as do other items. The same trends emerge in an analysis made by the United States Department of Agriculture of consumer purchases at different levels of income.[8] These studies indicated that although expenditures for formal education and recreation as a whole rise more rapidly than the average of all expenditures when income goes up, reading expenditures increase more slowly than the general average.

Thus, it would seem that to talk of a 50 percent increase over present public library expenditures by the end of the next decade is to talk in terms of possibilities rather than expectations based on established trends.

But the ultimate prospects for altering the present rates of increase between the public services so as to give the library a larger proportionate share are not entirely bleak. As we have analyzed them, the favorable factors are: an increase in the public library's organized political support, larger per capita incomes, more formal schooling, a larger percentage of urban-

[8] *Consumers Purchases Study*, Miscellaneous Publication, United States Department of Agriculture, Bureau of Home Economics, in Cooperation with the Works Progress Administration, 1940–41.

ism. Not only are per capita incomes increasing generally, but in some states, such as Florida and Texas, recent increases are so substantial that public library expenditures lag far behind the expectation of support that their per capita incomes justify. Over the country as a whole, too, a larger percentage of young people each year are completing eighth grade, high school, and college education. And more people are leaving the farms to move into urban or near-urban areas. Organized political effort under the leadership of librarians, moreover, is increasingly directed toward the development of rural library services and to the discovery of means of reducing artificial tax ceilings. If all these favorable factors could operate at a maximum of speed and effectiveness, the 50 percent increase of total public library expenditures would not be an impossible achievement. The probability of increase, however, is considerably less.

These calculations leave out of account two unpredictable factors in the present situation which may have a negative effect on the possibility of an increase of public library support. One is the growing concentration of national effort and income on the needs of defense and economic aid implied in the vigorous prosecution of the cold war and total diplomacy. In such an effort during the next decade, the more permanent, cultural needs of the people may receive low priorities. The second possibility is that the newer means of mass communication, especially television, may be introducing a trend counter to the increase of book reading and library use which have hitherto resulted from an up curve of formal schooling. The newer media may provide more and more of the information, ideas, and recreation for the available hours of leisure, so that book reading and library use will become more narrrowly limited as activities of both children and adults. As yet no such influence has been generally effective according to surveys of citizen time and attention in relation to the media of communication. For the present we may assume that during the next decade: considerable increase of public library income is possible; some increase is probable; unpredictable or uncontrollable factors will determine to some extent the amount of actual increase; but among the factors are the comprehensiveness and effectiveness of the organization of librarians themselves directed to increasing tax support for libraries on a state and local basis.

9

LIBRARY OPERATIONS

THERE ARE TWO WAYS of increasing the amount and quality of public library services. One is to increase income. The present sources of public library revenue and the more likely sources of increased income were described in the preceding chapter. The second way is to make changes in library operations or management which would result in more or better service with the same expenditure of money. This is not what usually passes for economy—that is, reduction of public funds appropriated for library purposes. Such action by officers of the general government may be necessary at times because of fiscal or economic stringency. But often the result is equivalent to reduction in public library service to the community, especially the quality of service. Changes to produce more efficient operations in the library field are not so likely to reduce total expenditures as to enable library personnel, without additional expenditures, to provide more materials and services in larger variety to more people. We need to explore this route to library economy.

THE NATURE OF LIBRARY OPERATIONS   An examination of what goes on in a public library reveals that a large part of the daily operations are repeated, routinized items of staff activity. These items are involved in the handling of library materials as physical objects: ordering, receiving, and preparing books for quick individual identification and use, moving them and recording their movements to and from the shelves and across circulation desks. Add to these activities the custody, maintenance, and repair of library equipment and books, and we have accounted for 60 percent of the 314 separable staff activities identified for us by librarians and more than 60 percent of the total staff time spent at work in the public libraries which co-operated in special Inquiry studies.

Library operations are by no means made up entirely of routinized, repeated items of work. A large part of some of the operations defined for us by librarians and substantial parts of others require highly qualitative judgments, specialized knowledge, broad intellectual background, skill in human relations, and overall administrative ability. But for effective management public libraries, like many other institutions, need to pay particular attention to discovering the best ways of organizing and performing a large number of small units of activity.

Like other institutions—especially those not under the constant spur of profit seeking—we might expect public library operations to be compounded of clear-cut, rational, economical processes and traditional, rule-of-thumb, wasteful practices never subjected to rigid analysis. This is the more likely because of the historical evolution of the public library. Its early leadership had a major background of interest and training in literary, cultural fields rather than in science, technology, and administration. The same tendency survives in the most of the present library personnel. Public libraries, as we have seen, have been developed as comparatively autonomous enterprises within the city government structure. Consequently, although they have escaped inefficiencies imposed by political patronage and the hampering uniformities of bureaucratic regulation, they have also been left outside the constructive studies of management and personnel characterizing recent municipal administration at its best. Then, too, most public libraries in the United States are small, independent units. Detailed analysis of operations to discover ways of saving tiny segments of time in performing repeated activities has seemed futile to the town and village librarians. And for them it is futile. Only when the number of items of activity is very large in a day's work do extremely small savings per item result in any significant economy.

Because of this background of public library organization and management, a general survey of operations by the Inquiry seemed important. It was recognized that the analysis of practices and processes is primarily a task for library practitioners. It was not to be expected that the Public Library Inquiry as an outside agency would discover specific formulae for more economical operations in particular areas of work. Rather, the purpose was to make some assessment of the present state of management analysis in libraries and to discover whether time, effort, funds, and machinery for studies by librarians aided by experts in management analysis might help to improve the quantity and quality of public library services in line with official library objectives.

PREVIOUS STUDIES OF OPERATIONS AND TECHNIQUES   Ever since the nineteenth-century inventors such as Dewey and Cutter, librarians have been concerned with processes, techniques, and operational problems. In the last three decades leadership in the analysis of processes has been assumed by committees of library specialists in particular fields organized usually under the aegis of the American Library Association. These committees of cataloguers, bibliographical specialists, children's librarians, and other groups have provided and are continuing to provide means to improved practices applicable to their respective fields. The limitations have been typical of all committees without full-time secretariat or research staff in which members contribute their time from the hours left over after their full-time positions. There have been some instances in which funds and personnel were made available for sustained intensive work, and these studies frequently paid off in significant advances in library methods and materials.

A second type of analysis has been the general survey of a single library or library system. Generally such surveys have consisted of brief, one- or two-man studies of an institution by librarians or library school faculty members of recognized ability and long experience. The benefits to the libraries studied have been real, and the survey reports have cumulated into a sizable literature of library organization and operation. But the demands of the specific situation have usually called for rough, overall analyses and immediately applicable, politically possible recommendations. Little attention has been paid to a more systematic approach involving the development of precise instruments usable for repeated and, therefore, comparative analyses. Consequently, the library survey has been limited as a means for general rationalization[1] of public library operations.

In isolated instances surveys applied to a single public library system have used techniques of detailed, precise measurement with regard to their technical processes or flow of work. The more precise studies frequently have tended to center around the mechanics and costs of cataloguing, and have been carried out mainly in university libraries. At least one major study, however, although specifically directed at cost accounting, was concerned with public library operations as a whole and involved the participation of thirty-seven public libraries in various parts of the country, most of them in the 25,000–100,000 population group. This was the Baldwin-Marcus study of 1939–1940.

The Public Library Inquiry began its work in this field with a review of the Baldwin-Marcus study and a canvass of

[1]The term "rationalization" is used here in its management rather than psychological connotation: i.e., the reduction of processes to consciously organized, highly rational activities rather than traditional, unanalyzed, rule-of-thumb operations.

the libraries involved in it, to determine what the results were in improved public library practice. The Baldwin-Marcus report itself drew attention sharply (1) to its finding that professional personnel in the libraries were frequently employed wastefully in clerical tasks and to the importance of job descriptions and training procedures related to actual work done as revealed by studies such as those carried on in the co-operating libraries; (2) to the possibilities of simplifying the processes of cataloguing, registration, circulation, and reference and the necessity of more exact measurement of the latter as a means of rational analysis leading to simplification. The report also urged public library administrators to accept responsibility for setting in motion a continuing review of library procedures. The Public Library Inquiry's canvass of the co-operating libraries indicated that about half of them had made some immediate use of the results of the study, mainly to reassign or redefine personnel or to simplify procedures. The replies were discouraging, however, with regard to the establishment of a policy and mechanism for a continuing review of library practices and procedures. Less than one in seven of the co-operating libraries had established such a policy. This was the more discouraging because all the libraries in the study had entered it voluntarily, had contributed funds and time to carry it out, and were all in places having populations of 25,000 or more.

The Baldwin-Marcus study, then, indicated that public libraries have much to gain from intensive, quantitative analyses of their procedures, but that the development of the will and the machinery to conduct such analyses on a continuing basis were not readily forthcoming.

THE INQUIRY STUDY OF LIBRARY OPERATIONS   The Inquiry's special study of public library operations, therefore, was centered upon devising a practicable means to encourage public library participation in intensive self-measurement and analysis. The aim was broadly exploratory, sampling all public library operations, not merely the technical processes, and sampling different sizes of libraries, not only the middle-size and large institutions which had hitherto been almost exclusively the objects of studies of technical and management processes.

By questionnaires to the sixty public libraries constituting the Inquiry's sample, followed by personal visits and observation in a number of libraries of different sizes, knowledge was gained regarding the existing methods and problems involved in carrying on technical library processes.

An intensive measurement was made in three public libraries of different sizes[2] of the time taken by every worker in the library for each of the many library activities, all the way from planning policies and programs through issuing borrowers' cards and selecting materials for groups, to cleaning, dusting, and maintaining buildings. In addition, a record was made of the time taken to perform separately identifiable units of work such as discharging a book, cataloguing an item, conducting a children's story hour, or shelving noncirculating material.

Preliminary to the recording of time and units of work a list of twenty major library operations was drawn up;[3] each

[2] The three libraries were included in the Inquiry sample. They were selected because they were known to be well-managed institutions, one from each of the three different size groups. The populations served were 430,000, 40,000, and 14,000, respectively. Unsuccessful attempts were made to include one of the very small libraries in the sample also, in the intensive study of operations. The failure, despite the willing co-operation of these smaller libraries in other aspects of the Inquiry, may be of some significance as to the likelihood of participation of small public library units in self-analysis of their operations without outside stimulation and guidance.

[3] The list as drawn up by the Inquiry specialist and the staff members of the three libraries made use of previous attempts to define the essential public library operations. The list finally agreed upon was: (1) Selection of Materials, (2) Acquisition of Materials, (3) Cataloguing and Classification, (4)

operation was divided into its constituent activities, and each activity was classified by the librarians according to its professional or nonprofessional character. Five hundred items were listed on the report form. The entire library personnel was prepared for the recording task by a series of four meetings at which discussion and criticism of the recording forms and explanation of the purposes of the study were shunted back and forth between department and branch chiefs, section heads, and workers in small units. There was also a trial period of recording. The two weeks of actual measurement were followed by a check up and review of the completed records in units and departments, a central tabulation, analysis, and report of results, and finally there were discussion and evaluation of the findings by the staff as a whole and by each of the major units.

THE DEVELOPMENT OF MACHINERY OF ANALYSIS   The object of this rather elaborate process of measurement in the three libraries was to build and test machinery for continuous analysis of operations within the libraries themselves. The study did require participation in planning and analysis by an outside management counsel, but he attempted to gain acceptance of his role as that of advisor and technical expert. The emphasis was on general participation of the library staff in the co-operative discovery of better ways of doing the library's

Mechanical Preparation and Processing of New Material, (5) Registration of Patrons, (6) Circulation, (7) Work with Children, (8) Work with Schools, (9) Information Services to Patrons, (10) Reference and Readers' Advisory Service to Patrons, (11) Work with Organizations and Groups of Patrons, (12) Preparatory Activities (examining new materials, reading professional literature, etc.), (13) General Administration, (14) Personnel Administration, (15) Publicity and Public Relations, (16) Binding and Repair of Materials, (17) Care, Operation, and Maintenance of Rooms, Buildings, and Grounds, (18) Printing (for library departments), (19) Security of Persons and Property, (20) Travel, Transportation, and Shipping. To these was added a twenty-first, or miscellaneous, category to include all time spent which was not subsumed under the twenty operations.

work and of developing a motivation which would result in staff acceptance of the results of measurement. It was attempted also to establish measurement and analysis of library operations as a regular, internal process carried on as one aspect of library administration rather than a task to be performed for libraries by outsiders, or for all libraries by any one library or at any one time.

Thus, the concrete result is a manual of tested forms, schedules, and procedures available for use by other public libraries and illustrated by results from three libraries rather than any general prescriptions of better ways of performing specific public library tasks. Indeed, a significant finding of the three-library analysis was that the diagnosis of particular operating wastes made by the time studies was different for each of the libraries. In one, the time measurements indicated excessive use of professionals at the circulation desk; in another the local preparation of catalogue cards was brought into question; in still another waste seemed to be in the personnel arrangements for physical maintenance of the branch buildings. The studies also provided the perspective gained from seeing the total distribution of staff time between the major library operations. Cataloguing, for instance, was found to occupy an average of 6 percent of total staff time as compared with physical maintenance or with circulation, each of which occupied 14 percent of staff time. Thus, although saving by more efficient cataloguing processes would undoubtedly be a useful gain, the amount might be much less than an improvement in physical maintenance activities or work economies at the circulation desk.

It was recognized that the time study and work unit measurement in the three libraries and the less intensive inquiries as to technical operations in the larger sample were preliminary and exploratory only. If public libraries become convinced that intensive measurement of operations is desirable, the study in a single library under expert management guidance would be only the first of at least three steps in a comprehensive program of rationalizing operations. The second step would be to enlist a number of public libraries of similar size and type in simultaneous self-analysis, using identical forms and procedures, and then to compare results so as to locate points of probable waste in each of the participating libraries. The third step would be the intensive study by a single library of specific points of probable inefficiency, or by the group of libraries if the points of probable waste in the libraries coincided. At this third stage outside industrial engineers or management experts might be called in as trained observers and diagnosticians to apply mechanization, standardization, improvement of layout, or work simplification. It is to be expected that in time the successive steps would be included as one of the regular processes of public library administration, with specific analysis applied to weak spots in the operating structure on the basis of recurring, overall, comparative studies of homogeneous groups of public libraries.

DIVERSITY OF SIZE AND PERSONNEL ANALYSIS   The Inquiry's analysis of library operations reinforced the conclusion based on its other studies that it is unreal to conceive of public library activities in overall terms about which one can generalize. Here, as elsewhere, it was found that libraries with staffs of 400, 40, 4, and 1 were not just telescoped or magnified replicas of each other. In operating procedures, as in services, they had such different characteristics that they could most usefully be studied as at least four different kinds of institution.

The need to group libraries by size for analysis was most obvious in the problem of allocating personnel to tasks appropriate to their ability, skills, and training. The desirability for such an allocation in public libraries based upon scientific job analysis, classification, and description was emphasized not only in the Inquiry's time studies, studies of personnel and of finance, but also in the Baldwin-Marcus and other previous surveys.

But the presence in a single library of a group of workers numerous enough to enable a division of labor to take place along lines of specialized ability occurred only in the Type I and Type II public libraries defined in Chapter 4 (public libraries serving populations of 25,000 or more). In the Type III libraries included in our sample (serving populations of 5,000 to 25,000), the professionals on the staff served as Jacks, or, more usually, Jills—of all library trades, performing some of the routine as well as professional library operations. In these libraries, also, the nonprofessionals assumed tasks which require professional education for their proper performance. And in the very small libraries (Type IV, serving populations of less than 5,000) nonprofessionals or half-trained professionals were performing all the library work.

This means that for two thirds of the country's public libraries—to some extent for nine tenths of them—studies designed to gain the efficiencies of division of labor according to specialized ability would be a waste of time. This must remain true as long as the one- or two-man village libraries remain isolated, self-contained units.

It only blurs the real picture to talk of numerical standards of administration or management applicable to all public libraries, such as the division of professional and nonprofessional staff on a fifty-fifty basis, which has been proposed in library literature. In the two larger libraries studied intensively by the Inquiry, the staff time spent in work of a professional nature was found to approximate 30 percent of the total staff time comprising the day's work. The amount of misassigned time[4] in these large libraries averaged 10 percent. It could hardly be reduced to zero in any working situation. Both institutions analyzed have an excellent reputation for skillful and thoroughly modern management, so that 40 percent of professional personnel might be thought of tentatively as a maximum for large libraries.

But this percentage could not be applied to the smaller public libraries. The Inquiry's time study in the Type III library (5,000–25,000 population) showed that more than 28 percent of professional staff time was spent on nonprofessional activities, and 15 percent of the time of nonprofessionals on professional activities. Obviously it was impossible for the libraries of this size to restrict the professional staff to professional duties.

Although the Inquiry was unable to conduct intensive time measurements in any very small public library (Type IV, under 5,000 population), our more general study of library personnel indicated that in these tiny institutions no line of distinction between professional and nonprofessional work existed. It could hardly exist when the staff consists of one or two persons only, neither of whom has had full professional training.

Even in the large public libraries, where scientific job analysis and allocation are feasible, the Inquiry's survey of personnel administration revealed that much still needs to be done to achieve maximum economy in relating people to tasks. Only half of the libraries in the Inquiry sample operated under a detailed organizational structure with lines of authority and function clearly established. In many there was a dearth of clearly-written manuals describing specific tasks and procedures for new and old workers. In less than half the libraries

[4]By misassigned time is meant the proportion of time that the professionals spend doing nonprofessional work or that nonprofessionals spend at professional tasks.

were positions classified, and there was a classification scheme in only two thirds of the larger (Type I and II) public libraries. Even in the libraries with position classification schemes, only 60 percent—24 percent of the whole number of libraries in the sample—had made a job analysis as a basis for the classification. A minority only had made studies of work loads. And only half the libraries of the sample had definite, published salary scales. Thus, it seems evident that despite the necessary restriction of studies to larger library units, job definition and classification are promising fields of analysis for increasing library efficiency.

FIELDS FOR FURTHER ANALYSIS   There were several other aspects of public library operation which as a result of the Inquiry and other studies seemed to be fruitful objects of further intensive, quantitative, comparative analysis.

One consists of the activities clustering around the circulation desk. It was found that some larger libraries had pioneered in introducing mechanization here with good results. Others, large and small, including county libraries, had put into effect time-saving work simplification. Still others had achieved savings in money and better use of time by reducing the number of man hours of professional personnel in circulation activities. But in many libraries circulation remained an uncriticized routine operation in which professional time was used wastefully.

A second process in which it appeared that intensive study might yield pay dirt was book selection. In most of the libraries sampled, selections were made by committees, panels, or by large numbers of individuals on the professional staff to whom specific titles had been assigned. There seem to have been purposes other than selection involved in the process, such as dissemination of knowledge of library materials and maintenance of morale by providing for participation in a preferred group activity. A few libraries had centralized the function of selection, with a resulting saving of professional man hours formerly devoted to the process. Whether there were losses in morale or in quality of the performance of the task could be determined only by detailed comparative studies.

The cataloguing process, in its various aspects, seemed to offer possibilities for further useful analysis, despite the concentrated attention it has received from the cataloguers themselves. Comparisons of practices of libraries in the sample brought to light anew these problems: the preparation of catalogue cards locally as compared with the use of Library of Congress and H. W. Wilson cards, of centrally-prepared cards for smaller libraries, similar to the Wilson cards, but covering more of the annual book output, and of the justification of some of the separate catalogues maintained by some public libraries, considering their cost. The public reaction to and use of the catalogue, almost completely neglected as a subject of inquiry by the libraries in our sample, deserves direct analysis.

The practice of some of the libraries of simplifying the whole handling of current ephemeral materials, including short-cuts in selection, purchase, cataloguing, classification, physical preparation, binding, shelving, and charging out, suggested that this is a fourth area that might yield constructive results from detailed analysis.

A fifth process for which practices had been revised or studies were under way in some libraries was the decision regarding the discard or storage of obsolescent materials, especially studies of the comparative costs of rebinding and repurchase, of removal of volumes to a central storage center versus transfer to storage shelves within the library. According to a long-term point of view, storage and discard seemed to be important matters in library building economy.

A sixth process that promised to benefit from analysis was

statistical recording and reporting. A number of the libraries studied seemed not to have made a really functional analysis of the statistical and other records kept currently or of the reports prepared periodically to see how directly they serve as instruments for administrative insights and control and for operational analysis. For instance, there was frequently a lack of full recording of reference services, especially of records which distinguish between items of information, reference, and research services. In a few libraries, however, the records and reports were carefully organized to aid administrative insight and control.

These six processes, along with job definition and allocation, are suggested for intensive analysis as a result of the studies of the Inquiry. Obviously they do not form a definitive list. They are familiar to librarians as areas in which efficiency might result from a direct attack. Other processes for which improvement is equally promising will appear as detailed measurements are applied to homogeneous groups of public libraries.

THE MEANS AND THE WILL FOR SELF-ANALYSIS   The question with which the Inquiry initiated its study of public library operations remains to be answered: that is, how can public libraries be encouraged to participate in self-measurement and analysis? To this question the Inquiry found no answer except to provide some tested tools and procedures which libraries might employ for self-analysis. The manual provides a direct aid for the libraries interested.

As was indicated above, self-measurement does require the guidance and the technical knowledge of experts in industrial or institutional engineering. For this an impetus might be provided by one or more of the library schools in the form of workshops in the techniques of scientific analysis of institutional operations, conducted by management experts for qualified librarians. At present, librarians so trained will be able to operate mainly in large city systems. But in time, as regional library systems develop, the trained administrative analyst would find a field very productive of results in serving from the state or regional center as a consultant and advisor to small library units within the region. These units now, it would seem from the Inquiry studies, are most in need of rationalizing their operations, but do not have the means of proceeding on their own to attack the problem. But even allowing for the impetus given to scientific analysis of library operations by the emergence of larger units of library service, the pressures for economy involved in seeking increased revenues from tax authorities, and the presence in library schools and the profession of persons qualified to conduct scientific analyses, the analyses themselves must be made and accepted by the rank and file of librarians. The problem of rationalizing operations, therefore, like other problems we have encountered in previous chapters, is closely bound up with the adequacy of the public library personnel, the subject of Chapter 10.

10

LIBRARY PERSONNEL
AND TRAINING

UP TO THIS POINT we have assumed that work in public libraries calls for professional skills and that there is a library profession. This was the assumption made when we were comparing the salaries of librarians with those in similar occupations, when we were classifying and measuring the activities that go to make up the library worker's day, and when we were assessing the possibilities of political persuasion possessed by library associations.

Not that all library work is professional! There are technical positions in the public library for which people need to be especially trained, but which are of a routine nature. There are clerical tasks, such as stenography, typewriting, filing, and the jobs of maintenance, custodianship, and transportation, all of which require specialized skills, but skills neither peculiar to library work nor of professional caliber. Two thirds of the work in the larger public libraries was found in our intensive analysis to be in these nonprofessional categories. The other third, however, consisted of staff activities of an administrative or specialized character calling for some degree of personal judgment and breadth or depth of intellectual background which led the librarians and our staff specialist in the study to classify them as professional. It would seem, then, that a realistic basis exists for a library profession.

WHAT IS A PROFESSION? But what do we mean by the term profession? There is no universally accepted definition which clearly marks off the professions from other occupations. A narrow definition would limit the term to the traditional, learned professions: medicine, law, and the ministry, all of which are based on intellectual disciplines and which involve a responsible, personal relation of the practitioner to the people served. But the high prestige of these older professions has led to the appropriation of the term by other occupations such as teaching, architecture, engineering, and journalism, whose skills are also based on intellectual disciplines. More recently, advertisers, undertakers, chiropodists, dancing masters, cosmetologists, and other self-conscious occupational groups have clamored for the dignity and status conferred by the professional title.

Although some of the latter groups make strange bedfellows for doctors, lawyers, and preachers, probably every organized occupation has some characteristics of a profession. Accepting this fact, the dictionary definitions of the term have made it synonymous with occupations in general. It seems useful for the analysis of the place and function of occupational groups in our society, however, to maintain a distinction between professions and the more inclusive categories covering all vocations.

The distinction is that a profession possesses specialized, communicable techniques based upon: (1) prolonged intellectual training; (2) a content of training that includes generalizations or principles; (3) the application of the principles in concrete professional practice, a complex process requiring the exercise of disciplined, individual judgment. To put it in another way, the specialized methods acquired in professional training always include something more than rule-of-thumb procedures or routinized skills. This may be held to be a definition of learned professions rather than all professions. But it is broad enough to include professions other than the three traditionally associated with the term, and it excludes many

useful, skilled occupations which do not depend on understanding and discipline in the application of formally-organized bodies of knowledge of a high degree of generality.

The common intellectual character of the professions has
given rise to similar professional activities and attitudes which
help to distinguish them from other occupations. That each
must have a long period of formal intellectual preparation has
led them to organize professional schools built either on top of
the collegiate structure or included in the instruction leading
to a combined professional and bachelor's degree. Because of
the basic character of the intellectual disciplines comprising
professional training, professional schools, for the most part,
have been included as constituent parts of universities. Being
placed in universities alongside graduate schools devoted to
the advancement of knowledge in special fields through research and inquiry, the professional schools, also, have become
in many cases centers of inquiry as well as of instruction in
the practices of the profession and the intellectual disciplines
underlying it. Thus, a rough way of identifying the professions is to locate those occupations which are entered through
professional schools in universities, professional schools where
inquiry is combined with instruction in the professional field.

A second kind of activity common to the professions is
organization of their members into professional associations
exercising a considerable degree of leadership and regulatory
authority in professional matters. By accreditation of its professional schools, the professional association, or some agency
related to it, sets minimums for the type and quality of education for the profession. By setting standards for admission to
its own organized groups, by influencing the form and content
of examinations or certification for entrance to professional
practice, the professional association largely determines who
shall be recognized as having professional status. By formal
codes or informal standards of conduct the professional organi-

zation possesses a continuing influence on professional practice, whether the codes are enforced by judicial process, formal disapproval and ostracism, or the force of prevailing professional opinion. In a few professions this machinery for the regulation of training, admission, and practice amounts to a legalized membership monopoly of the professional function. In most, however, the self-regulating activities constitute looser lines of guidance and influence. The degree to which the community delegates self-regulation to a professional group seems to depend on the complexity, and thus the esoteric character, of the process of applying principle to specific cases combined with general recognition of the social importance of the function which the profession performs.

The characteristics and activities common to the professions give rise, also, to similarities in attitude. The high degree of skill, painfully acquired by long training, develops in almost all professionals a strong group identification and pride. It tends to breed, also, a possessive or exclusive attitude toward nonprofessionals who attempt to invade the sphere of professional knowledge and activity. Finally, all professions preach, and to an extent their members practice, a primary obligation of loyalty to professional standards, even at the expense of financial gain. The high status and prestige achieved by the older learned professions may stem partly from this attitude, or "myth," of professionals in performing their services, dramatized as it is by the Hippocratic oath, the priest performing the last rites, or the judicial assignment of counsel to defend the penniless client.

The characteristics, activities, and attitudes described above are by no means exclusively professional. The craftsman and artist, the business man, the trade unionist, the conscientious mother, the telephone girl at her switchboard in time of flood or panic are characterized by one or more of them in high degree. But in our society they together form a complex which enables us to distinguish groups possessing them from occupations as a whole. And possessed by a group they tend to be substantial advantages in terms of status and prestige, as well as of effective performance of specialized social tasks.

LIBRARIANSHIP AS A PROFESSION   To what extent is librarianship a profession as here defined? Certainly, some of the specialized library techniques are based upon prolonged intellectual training. But the intellectual content of the training consists of acquaintance with the whole range of knowledge rather than the one or two fields of science or learning usually underlying other professions. Thus, it is frequently said that librarianship is a specialization in generalism. The specialization, however, includes development of skill and judgment in selecting, organizing, classifying, and bringing to focus for ready use, the recorded knowledge in the major fields. Paradoxical as is the librarian's intellectual specialization, therefore, it calls for prolonged training, possesses intellectual content, and involves complex judgments in applying general knowledge to specific uses.

Recognition of the professional character of the librarian's tasks in book selection, bibliography, reference, and guidance in the use of materials has been obscured by the fact that most libraries are so small that the librarian is obliged to combine these duties with the simpler technical processes involved in preparing, arranging, transporting, recording, and circulating materials. The small size of the majority of libraries has also delayed recognition of the professional character of administration and supervision in large library units.

Librarians engage in activities which are like those of professional groups. They have created a system of formal training in organized schools. But as we shall see below, the duration and character of library school training vary all the way from an undergraduate semester of simple technical courses taught by library staff members on a part-time basis to one or more full years of work beyond the baccalaureate with a full-time faculty of university caliber. The academic connections of the library training units also vary greatly. Library training units are to be found in separate vocational institutes, teachers colleges, liberal arts colleges, and in universities where they enjoy a formal status identical with the older professional schools. In the universities, however, with one or two exceptions, the library schools are much smaller in size and in facilities for research than are the other professional schools.

Like other professional groups, also, librarians, as we have seen, are organized into professional associations. Unlike some of the professions, however, no definite qualification other than interest in, or work in, libraries is set up for full association membership. An agency of the library association accredits library schools, but, as we shall see later, has not been able to establish any appreciable minimum standards of resources or performance. Furthermore, a large number of institutions training persons for libraries in schools are not accredited by the professional librarian's agency. Certification of librarians as a necessary preliminary to practicing the profession exists, but is much more limited in extent and effectiveness than accreditation. In fact, for the country as a whole certification exists as yet only in a token sense. Partly as a cause and partly as a consequence of lack of enforceable certification and accreditation, we found no definite lines of job classification and description which identify the professional positions in many public libraries. As we have seen in previous chapters, such lack of classification goes back to the basic difficulty of small public library units in which specialization of function is not possible. Thus, the regulatory activities of the professional librarians exist, but only in a rather undeveloped form.

We found librarians to be distinguished by attitudes which are like those of other professional groups. They have a sense of common occupational identity and pride. From library school teaching and the leadership groups there have been formulations and examples of professional standards of conduct, especially the concept of democratic public service, which have had an identifiable influence on the general membership. With regard to freedom of access to books and other materials, the professional association has drawn up a formal code, with a committee to aid librarians to resist pressures from groups attempting improper censorship of public library purchases and holdings. Although one detects, also, the usual sense of professional exclusiveness, the very indefiniteness of qualification for the professional category has resulted in a more hospitable attitude to interlopers than prevails in the more tightly organized professions.

Librarians, then, are not at present clearly defined or fully organized as a professional group. Perhaps they may best be categorized as a skilled occupation on its way to becoming an organized profession. It appears from reading the official literature, at least, that like other occupations the librarians have accepted professional status as a goal and are consciously seeking the prestige and authority which comes from academic and community recognition of that status. It is with this assumption that we shall review the findings of the Public Library Inquiry with regard to the characteristics, organization, and training of the personnel now occupying professional positions in public libraries.

PERSONAL CHARACTERISTICS   Our study of librarian characteristics was carried on by asking the professional personnel in the Inquiry's sample to fill out and return elaborate occupational questionnaires, personality inventory and vocational interest blanks. More than 3,000 of them, 84 percent of the whole number, did so, thus providing the basis for a representative profile of the professional workers in the country's libraries which are large enough to provide full-time positions on a professional level. Because of the lack of similar detailed inventories of occupational groups, comparisons with the professions and other occupations were limited to crude overall norms for the general population. But we are provided with a picture of what librarians in the aggregate are like.

The findings established a solid factual base for correcting the caricatures of the profession that have arisen from the almost universal human tendency to assume the existence of general occupational characteristics from a few exceptional cases. Librarians have been pictured frequently as acidulous old maids, timid, retiring bookworms, or sweet impractical idealists, as masculine women and feminine men. The Inquiry findings lead to the conclusion that as a group librarians have backgrounds, interests, and temperaments normal for persons engaged in the intellectual occupations. The men are reasonably masculine in their interests, the women are feminine. No unusual percentage of neurotics or ill-tempered people was revealed by the personality inventory. Present-day librarians were found to be recruited mainly from native American stock; from families with better than average formal education and occupational status. They seek to perpetuate their good educational backgrounds in their choice of husbands or wives. Many librarians are married; most would like to be. A number have been divorced, but a smaller proportion than in the whole population. Like others in intellectual occupations with modest pecuniary rewards, they tend to marry later and to have smaller families than does the average American adult. Their political attitudes and preferences are well within the broad middle range of liberal to conservative.

Like most other occupational groups, librarians say that they like their occupation and entered it because they thought it would be congenial to their interests. They would recommend their calling to their nephews and nieces. They join clubs, go to church, attend meetings, read newspapers, listen to the radio in roughly similar proportions to their neighbors in the places where they live and work. Exception may be noted, however, in the librarian's inclination to take a busman's holiday when off duty by reading books and serious magazines. But in this they probably do not deviate greatly from other occupations which deal so extensively with books. The personality inventories also showed some deviation of librarians from the norms established for young college graduates, in that librarians have somewhat less of a tendency to social ascendancy, aggressive leadership, and self-confidence. But, again, it is not clear whether this deviation would also hold for persons in similar occupations with work largely of a sedentary nature, performed in a quiet, friendly atmosphere, relatively free from the pressures and sharp personal rivalries for position and power that characterize much of commercial enterprise. The present public librarians as persons, then, seem to possess no handicaps to organization as a professional group, with professional interests and loyalties, toward which the community in time would accord the recognition due to professional status.

EDUCATIONAL AND ECONOMIC STATUS   When we turn to the public librarian's educational and economic status the picture is not so favorable. As reported in Chapter 8, the Inquiry's cross section of the librarians now in professional positions showed that only 58 percent held a bachelor's degree from an undergraduate college, only 40 percent had had a year of professional training. Thus, less than three fifths of the present library personnel defined as professional have achieved the minimum formal education required for regular status in any of the organized, learned professions, and only two fifths have met the minimum standard of preparation set by the librarians themselves for professional positions. This unfavorable picture is modified somewhat by the Inquiry finding that the proportions of librarians holding bachelor's and professional degrees increase as we measure the younger age groups in the profession.

The economic status of the present professional librarians, as we have seen in Chapter 8, is also unfavorable to the achievement of professional status. The median salary in the Inquiry sample, where the average length of service was seventeen years, was $100 less than the $2,800 annual minimum recommended by the American Library Association for beginners on the professional level. Except for a small group of public library administrators in larger cities, the salary range from the beginning to the end of the average professional library career was from less than $2,000 to $4,000 a year. Many people in the United States live on this economic level, but it is not a level likely to provide the living standards which are suited to continued professional growth. The average earnings of all factory workers are now a little over $3,000 a year.

Some of the older professions, such as teaching and the ministry, have compensated somewhat for low salary levels by security programs for accident, illness, and old age. But no similar provisions of general application have yet been established in the public library field. Certainly incentives other than pecuniary attract people to the library career and keep them in it. Love of books and libraries and the satisfaction of performing a useful public service were the principal reasons given by the librarians for entering and remaining in public library work. These are sound professional motives, but the economic rewards are such that the status tends to be a kind of shabby gentility rather than professional or financial security.

In another important respect the typical public library salary scale fails to provide a satisfactory professional career. As was pointed out in Chapter 8, the salary ladder progresses with very small upward steps to a certain point, then leaves vacant rungs from the middle administrative positions to two top rungs occupied by a chief librarian and assistant librarian. The result is that in the line of promotion an entering librarian may reasonably expect, in time, to reach a position as division and department head or top specialist. But the salaries are not graded so that the highest posts under the administrative chiefs will represent a reasonably satisfactory career line as far as salary goes. This failure to grade salaries up the ladder to the top on the basis of skill and experience is complicated by the fact that for socio-cultural or other reasons men are pre-ferred for the top administrative posts in public libraries. Thus, for the women who compose nine tenths of the present profes-sional personnel the career route so far as salary is concerned almost invariably reaches a dead end at a low level. This is not true, as our studies revealed, for the minority of men who en-ter library work. They start at the same point, but rise more rapidly and rise further—so that actually there is a dual career structure in the public library field, one for men and one for women. For both sexes, however, the present economic status of professional librarians is unfavorable to the recognition of professional status.

PROFESSIONAL AFFILIATIONS   So far as professional affili-ations are concerned, our studies of the librarians in the Inquiry sample indicated a measurable feeling of professional identity. Three fourths of the professional group belonged to the American Library Association, three fifths to a state asso-ciation. Local professional groups have not been organized in many places, so that the proportion who belong to them is not significant as a test of professional identity. Less than a fifth of the group attended the national library conventions; a third attended state and local library meetings. Only a small proportion of the librarians in the sample, an eighth or less, felt that professional associations were helpful to them. When asked their opinion on three major issues in the public library field (larger units of service, Federal aid, state certification) only about a half of the professional librarians had any opinion on them. Whether these indications of active affiliation with librarians as an organized profession reveal more or less identification than prevails in other professional groups is impossible to say because of the lack of comparative data. When we keep in mind the fact that library association membership and activity are an expression of the librarian's professional or personal interest and free choice, not a requirement for professional certification or status, and when we consider also the deterrent that dues and distance must be to participation for librarians on low salary levels, the percentages do not seem strikingly low.

An internal comparison of participation and attitude among the librarians in our sample gives further indication of the existence of professional identity. In the Inquiry sample 20 percent of the whole number above nonprofessional grades were classified by their libraries as subprofessional rather than professional. Whereas the professionals reported that in accepting their present posts they were strongly motivated by the reputation of the library for giving good service and by the opportunities offered for professional advancement, the subprofessionals reported that they had been interested in obtaining a position with a satisfactory work schedule and friendly, pleasant co-workers. More than half the professionals said that library work contributes more to their satisfaction and enjoyment in life than does any other interest or activity; less than a fifth of the subprofessionals reported such professional interest. A much smaller percentage of the subprofessionals than of the professional group were members of the professional associations, attended their meetings, and had opinions about major professional issues. Thus, among the library staff members holding positions which require library skills there was a clearly distinguishable group with professional interests and affiliations, as compared with the more personal interests in pay, work conditions, and associations which characterize hosts of workers in occupations not defined as professional.

SUBPROFESSIONAL OR NONPROFESSIONAL SPECIALISTS   The work, interests, and attitudes of the subprofessionals in the Inquiry sample were such as to give them a closer affiliation with the clerical than with the professional personnel. Rather than a term defining a clear-cut occupational group, "subprofessional" proved to be an anomalous label applied differently in different library systems. Some library administrators, coming to this conclusion, have proposed that the subprofessional category be eliminated entirely from the pattern of personnel classification. If the librarians are seeking a sharper definition and organization of professional library personnel, the proposal deserves favorable consideration.

Subprofessionals are not to be confused with the small number of subject-matter specialists found in larger libraries who have advanced training and degrees in academic subjects. For some purposes such specialists have to be given designations that differ from those used for librarians with professional school training. We found that in a number of libraries they were simply given a nonprofessional status. Others, more realistically, have included these highly professional experts in the general professional category, designating them as specialists rather than librarians.

Whether called subprofessional or nonprofessionals, however, there is a group of workers in public libraries performing the simpler, specialized tasks. They are distinguished from the clerical workers in that their skills are peculiarly library skills rather than clerical skills used generally in institutions of all kinds. Proper training for their tasks, therefore, is a concern of librarians.

At present there is even less uniformity in academic requirements and training for these nonprofessional technicians[1] than for the professional personnel. We found that a few library schools give an undergraduate sequence of courses in library techniques along with regular work in the arts and sciences leading to the bachelor's degree. Those completing this four-year program are given the title of subprofessional librarians. Some library administrators have proposed a similar program of training in library techniques, along with other academic work, for junior college students, who would be given a nonprofessional status in libraries as technicians. In most cases at present, however, training for the simpler library techniques is done in libraries by apprenticeship or by more formal methods of instruction while on the job. Clerical workers with aptitude and interest have been recruited for these technical library jobs. A number of librarians, in fact, have taken the position that there is no need to distinguish nonprofessional technicians or specialists from the general clerical personnel and that the technicians can be recruited and prepared adequately for their tasks by in-service training.

The present divergence of views among experienced librarians with regard to this matter will probably be lessened only when scientific job analysis and definition have been extended widely enough to make clear the exact nature, difficulty, and intellectual content of the technical library jobs. Our analysis and observations indicate that the outcome is likely to be: (1) that the skills will be most economically tested by general written and performance tests based on in-service or junior

---

[1]For want of a better word, technician is used here to denote this group of workers. In terms of similar types of work in other professions it is an appropriate title. Unfortunately, in librarianship the term technical has been used to describe some of the more mechanical library processes in which there is work of both professional and nonprofessional grade.

college preparation rather than by extended formal higher education; (2) that transfer from the clerical to the technical category will be made easy on the basis of such tests; (3) that transfer from the technical to the professional category will be effected only by completion of the academic and professional library school education required for professional certification; (4) that scientific job analysis and enlargement of library service areas will result in transferring many library tasks from the professional to the nonprofessional-technical category.

CLERICAL AND MAINTENANCE PERSONNEL   The clerical and maintenance personnel in public libraries can be distinguished from both professional and nonprofessional technical personnel in that their skills are not applicable to library operations only. Stenographers, typists, bookkeepers, filing clerks, maintenance, custodial, and transportation workers possess special techniques needed by libraries as well as many other public and private organizations. For such employees a job in a public library is primarily a typist's or janitor's job; only secondarily a library job. In the progress of their careers they may move in and out of library positions to similar positions in banks, factories, schools, or government agencies without loss of experience or salary ratings. Although they are an important part of the public library's staff, their recruitment for training and their training itself are conducted by institutions outside the control of the library profession. The availability of competent workers, their salaries, and their working conditions are governed to a large extent by conditions in the local labor market.

PERSONNEL MANAGEMENT   The quantity and the quality of the work performed by clerical and maintenance workers as well as by the other members of the library staff, however, are primarily matters of personnel management of concern to every chief librarian. The Inquiry made a special study of this aspect of personnel organization and practice by means of questionnaires filled out by the directing staffs of fifty-eight of the sixty public libraries of various sizes and types constituting the Inquiry sample. In addition, visits and direct observation of existing practices and facilities were made in many of these libraries.

The findings corresponded with those reported in Chapter 9 with regard to management analysis in general. In small libraries job supervision was on a personal rather than a systematic basis, varying from petty tyranny and wasteful disorder to a high state of morale, efficiency, and congeniality under the head librarian. The conclusion from our observations of the smaller libraries in the sample was that although in them personnel management must remain personal and informal, more rather than less systematic procedures would be desirable in such matters as definition and allocation of duties, supervision of work, arrangements for vacations and retirement.

The findings revealed also less systematic personnel administration than might be expected in many of the larger public libraries employing hundreds of people. In the larger public libraries it was found that more responsibility for personnel administration was delegated to a special officer. In a number of them, however, no separate personnel offices with full-time personnel had been established. Where they do exist, they have developed within recent years. In very few of the libraries were the personnel offices in the hands of people with specialized training or experience for their tasks. Furthermore, in a number of instances the library executives seemed unaware of the significance of modern personnel practices or of the value of a personnel office under especially trained leadership.

The results of this lag in adequate top office organization were reflected in the actual patterns of personnel management.

In Chapter 9 it was pointed out that in most cases the libraries in the Inquiry sample had failed to relate people to jobs economically through basic position classification schemes made and revised after detailed job analyses. In Chapter 8 the lack of salary scales directly related to the level of difficulty and responsibility of each position and the absence of general provisions for financial security were noted. The Inquiry's survey of personnel practices also revealed a frequent lack of modern procedures developed by personnel experts in local recruiting, selection, assignment, evaluation of work, in-service training, and provision for employee vacations, payment for overtime, and other working conditions.

Ten of the sixty libraries in the Inquiry sample were under the jurisdiction of city or state civil service commissions. This meant that for these libraries the procedures of selection, appointment, promotion, and salary grades and job classification were to a large extent imposed upon them by an outside agency. A certain amount of systematization and uniformity were in this way guaranteed. But although libraries in the sample under civil service commissions were more favorably disposed to them than those who were not, there was considerable objection to the delays, red tape, artificial uniformity and impersonality of civil service procedures. It is impossible to separate the librarians' traditional attitudes favoring autonomy within the municipal government from their rational criticism of the inadequacies in administration of the merit system which undoubtedly exist in many places. At any rate, many librarians question whether the personnel practices introduced by civil service commissions will result in real improvement of personnel management. Very few cases were found in which a strong public library personnel office was co-operating with a progressive civil service commission to adapt the commission's procedures to library needs and requirements and to decentralize its administration in library hands. This, however, rather than impotent opposition, may be the only road to improvement, inasmuch as the merit system has become a fixed part of local governmental machinery from whose jurisdiction public libraries are not likely to be exempt in larger proportion than is now the case.

The Inquiry attempted to discover how far public libraries have in practice incorporated the most recent developments in personnel theory and research. Information was sought especially on the function of staff associations, trade unions, and other devices of two-way communication between top office and workers on all levels in voicing grievances, requests and suggestions, and in presenting and discussing policies and programs. There were questions also to discover how sensitive library management has become to the composition and leadership of each of its small working groups so as to establish maximum satisfactions and loyalties arising from congenial group relations. The findings here were more negative than for the orthodox procedures designed to create a systematic, orderly, equitable machinery of personnel administration. Few librarians in the sample were aware of the significance of these newer canons of personnel management, and fewer had put them into full practice in their libraries. Here, as elsewhere, it seemed evident that public libraries have not yet developed fully the agencies or the patterns for the execution of modern personnel policy.

EVOLUTION OF PROFESSIONAL LIBRARY SCHOOLS   The belated development of modern personnel programs in public libraries, like other deficiencies in current library operations, reflects to some extent the kind of formal training provided for librarians in the last generation. With the exception of four institutions established shortly before 1900, separately organized library schools began to prevail for training librarians around the turn of the century. Thus, the training of the staff members now in public libraries covers almost the entire span of library school existence. Instruction in the ways of librarianship, of course, did not begin as late as this. But before 1900 most librarians learned their trade by direct apprenticeship in libraries or by training classes conducted in libraries by the library staff members.

The first library school outside of a library was set up by Melvil Dewey as a unit in Columbia University, but it had a very close connection with the university library. Dewey's purpose was to establish a generally accessible training class in library techniques rather than a professional school integrated into the academic system. As he put it, the training was designed to give "the best obtainable advice, with specific suggestions on each of the hundreds of questions which arise from the time a library is decided to be desirable till it is in perfect working order, including the administration."[2] The instruction did not differentiate between major problems of book selection and minor skills such as filing, shelving, handwriting, and typewriting. The early library schools, in short, were trade schools, not professional schools. Of the fourteen schools established before 1920, only three started in universities; the eleven others were located in libraries, vocational institutes, or vocational colleges. These early schools set the curriculum pattern for the year or less of special training for librarianship—a pattern which has survived in part down to the present.

A definite break from the philosophy and purpose of the existing library schools, however, was made in the early 1920's with the publication of the report by C. C. Williamson on library education, under the sponsorship of the Carnegie Corporation.[3] Williamson's report and later program as head of

[2]The source for the Dewey plans and for the quotation is Ernest J. Reece, *The Curriculum in Library Schools*, New York, Columbia University Press, 1936, pp. 31–32.

[3]See Charles C. Williamson, *Training for Library Service*, New York, Carnegie Corporation, 1923, 165 pp.

the library school at Columbia University definitely set the librarians on the road to the education of an organized profession as defined earlier in this chapter. He urged librarians to recognize two types of library work—one professional, the other clerical—and he held that library schools should confine themselves to training of the professional type. For proper professional training he recommended: (1) affiliation of all library schools as departments or schools of universities, similar to the relationship established for other professional schools; (2) full use of the university's scholarly resources to enrich and broaden the content of the curriculum; (3) building of the library school program on the post-bachelor level, with the bachelor's degree required for entrance; (4) a three-year program, consisting of one year of instruction in basic subjects, a year of specialized training, with one year of library experience intervening; (5) provision for continued professional education for librarians in service in summer schools and institutes.

The Williamson program for transforming library technical schools into effective instruments for the education of a profession set the direction of change and improvement which has continued until now. There were some modifications of his prescription: the two years of formal instruction were compressed into two semesters, and the idea of a period of internship before award of the professional degree did not take hold. The ALA, acting on another of Williamson's recommendations and aided by Carnegie Corporation funds, early in the twenties created an agency to set standards for library education and to accredit only such schools as met them. By 1936 Louis Wilson, head of the Chicago Graduate Library School established by Carnegie funds on a graduate basis, reviewing the changes of a decade and a half, reported that many of the Williamson recommendations were a long way on the road to accomplishment. But the elevation of library education to a truly professional level, with graduate-professional library schools comparable in standards and resources to the university schools training for the older professions, has by no means been achieved even yet.

At the time the Public Library Inquiry reviewed the programs and resources of the library schools (1948–49) they were in the midst of a major transition in degree structure, instructional plans, accreditation policy, and standards. Nevertheless, an inventory was made with the idea of providing a quantitative picture of tendencies as well as present status. Data were obtained mainly from a questionnaire filled out and returned by the directors of the thirty-four accredited library schools in the United States, from another questionnaire returned by all but one of the 220 faculty members giving full-time or part-time instruction in the schools, and from a third set of questionnaires filled out by the chief officers of eight large universities which provided figures on salaries, budgets, faculty, students, and other items for all the professional schools, including the library schools in the eight universities.

THE DIVERSITY OF ACADEMIC LEVELS AND AFFILIATIONS   A major finding from these data and from other available material is that the thirty-four library schools, despite formal accreditation, vary greatly in size, academic position, and instructional resources. Before the recent changes in programs and degrees and the moratorium on accreditation, the library schools were officially classified into three types: (1) thirteen offered a year of library training as part of an undergraduate curriculum leading to the bachelor's degree; (2) twenty-three offered the year's library training only after completion of work for the AB or BS degree, but awarded a professional bachelor's degree at its completion; (3) four of the twenty-three awarded a professional master's degree for a second year of post-bachelor library instruction, and one offered both the master's and the doctor's professional degrees.

There was a similar diversity in the academic affiliation of the library schools. The five offering degrees beyond the professional baccalaureate were all located in major universities of high standing. But five of the others requiring the AB or BS for admission to library training were not in universities at all. Rather, they were in technical institutes, vocational colleges, or undergraduate colleges for women. And of the thirteen offering library training on the undergraduate level four were in teacher-training institutions rather than general colleges or universities, and several in universities were included in departments or schools of education. To add to the diversity, outside the schools accredited by ALA there were at least four times as many library training centers located in teachers' colleges or schools of education in universities. The library training in these institutions was oriented to school libraries, the schools were accredited by educational bodies, and the librarian-trained graduates were certified as librarians in schools.

THE SIZES OF LIBRARY SCHOOLS   Between the thirty-four accredited library schools there were great differences in the sizes of their student bodies and faculties. The nearly 2,000 students enrolled in 1948–49 were distributed among the schools very unevenly, three schools enrolling between ten and twenty each, and two at the other end of the scale with 171 and 261, respectively. The major characteristic of the group as a whole, however, was smallness. Nearly a third of the schools each enrolled less than enough to fill an average-size classroom; almost half had enrollments under forty; the median size of the student body was forty-six. There were no recent, exact figures available for enrollments in the unaccredited library training centers, but the earlier figures indicate that their median enrollment was even smaller than for the accredited schools.

These small enrollments are to be compared with much larger student bodies prevailing in the other university professional schools. The average size of the student body of the library schools in five of the eight universities providing figures was smaller than any of the other professional schools, next to smallest in two others, third from the bottom of the ten different professional schools in the other. The library schools' average of 98 in the eight institutions was much smaller than the average of 822 for the sixty-six professional schools in the sample.

Limiting the comparison of enrollments to the four professions in which women predominate, we find that in the eight universities the schools of nursing had average enrollments two and one half times larger, schools of social work three times larger, and schools of education fifteen times larger than the averages for the library schools. Omitting the professional schools in the sample which admit large numbers of undergraduates (business, education, and engineering), the normal range of the professional school enrollments appears to be 200 to 600 with a median at 300. If library schools had average student bodies of 300, seven schools could accommodate all the students now distributed in the thirty-four institutions.

With student bodies so small, it is not surprising that the faculty groups in library schools should also be small. Although 220 persons were engaged in instruction in the accredited library schools during 1948–49, nearly 60 percent of them were on a part-time basis. The equivalent of part-time and full-time instructors in terms of full-time teaching load was 133. The average per school of actual full-time faculty members was three; on the basis of full-time equivalence the average was five.

This average for all the library schools, however, conceals the great variation between them in the size of their instructional staffs. As early as 1921 Williamson set a minimum of four faculty members on full-time as necessary for the proper staffing of a professional library school. Less than this would mean that instructors would have to do double duty on the major subjects of school instruction. The five schools offering advanced degrees were above this minimum, having an average of six actual full-time teachers, eight on the basis of full-time equivalence. But the other schools on the post-bachelor level averaged two full-time instructors, four on the basis of full-time equivalence; the accredited undergraduate library schools averaged only one full-time teacher, two on the basis of full-time equivalence.

A standard frequently used for measuring numerical adequacy of instruction staff at all academic levels is the ratio of students to teachers. For the thirty-four library schools this ratio is fourteen to one. It is higher and therefore less favorable than the ten to one norm proposed for post-bachelor instruction by the President's Commission on Higher Education; and the library school's ratio for full-time faculty members is nearly twice as high as the average in a group of colleges and universities of high standing, with less than 1,200 students enrolled.[4] The average library school ratio, however, in the eight universities was lower and more favorable than the average for all the professional schools in the group; it was considerably lower than the average for the very large professional schools on the undergraduate level in these universities.

More important than overall comparisons are the differences in ratio of students to faculty among the thirty-four

[4] See report of Committee on the Economic Status of the Profession, "Instructional Salaries in Forty-two Selected Colleges and Universities for the Academic Year 1948–49," *American Association of University Professors Bulletin*, XXXIV (winter, 1948), 778–797.

library schools themselves. There were two schools having student bodies of fourteen each and teaching staffs of two and three, respectively, only one of whom in each case was on a full-time basis; there was one school with eighteen students and a faculty of three full-time and one part-time member; another with twenty-three students and a faculty of nine, only one of whom was full-time. At the other extreme from these tiny schools with ratios of four, five, six, or seven to one, was a student body of 171 taught by one full-time and two part-time teachers, a ratio of sixty-eight to one; a student group of forty-five, with a student-faculty ratio of thirty-seven to one; another of fifty-eight, with a ratio of twenty-seven to one.

Evidently there are in library schools two different factors, each of which gives the student-faculty ratio a different significance. In some schools with limited budgets and sizable student bodies the school's administration has failed to hire enough faculty members for the teaching task. Other library schools have student bodies so small that, as the very low student-faculty ratios indicate, the units are inherently uneconomical and there are too few faculty members to provide the specialized expertness in each subject desirable for education on a professional level. The relatively small size of library schools is not due to lack of physical capacity. The reports to the Inquiry showed that the existing accredited library schools had room for about half again more students than were currently enrolled.

FACULTY EDUCATIONAL AND ECONOMIC STATUS   What about the academic status and income of the 220 persons (36 percent men and 64 percent women) composing the staffs of the accredited library schools? Compared with the professional staffs in the eight universities, the number of library school teachers possessing advanced degrees, the proportion in the higher professorial ranks, the range and average of salaries, and the extent of professional experience in libraries fall a little below the middle position for the whole group of professional schools. The library schools were distinctly below the median for the staffs of the schools training for the older professions, but on a higher level than the staffs of the schools of the newer professions, especially those professions which, like librarianship, are predominantly feminine in membership and whose members do not receive on the average higher salaries than those in the prevailing academic salary scales. The median library school salary in 1949, $4,200, was approximately $1,500 higher than for the professional librarians in the Inquiry sample, although top positions in public and university libraries were higher than top library school posts. When the library school salaries were compared with the levels of rank and salary for the faculties in a group of colleges and universities selected for their high standing, the library school faculty averages fell below those in the selected institutions. But even here the library schools were not in a markedly inferior position—one that could not be remedied by positive action within a decade.

As regards other elements of faculty occupational status, such as permanent tenure, provisions for retirement, travel, and sabbatical leave—the returns from the library schools indicated that their staffs share equally in these important matters with the other faculty members in the institutions of which they are a part.

A similar approximation to equality is revealed in the comparison of library school budgetary resources with the general averages for all professional schools. Students of academic administration have stated that the amount spent by an institution per student for instruction supplies "as accurate a means of educational standards as is available in terms of numerical symbols or money values. They are, therefore, in a very real sense, the critical figures, though they cannot measure such intangible and variable factors as devotion to teaching in spite of material handicap on the one hand, or distraction and inefficiency on the other."[5]

By this yardstick the average expenditure for instruction per student in the thirty-four library schools, $390, was found to be $23 less than in the selected group of colleges of high standing; and in the eight universities the average for instruction per student in library schools was $21 less than for all the professional schools in these universities. Thus, the library schools seem not to be far below the general average of professional schools or colleges in instruction expense per student. As was pointed out earlier in connection with student-faculty ratios, there seem to be two factors at work in different institutions: an uneconomically small number of students and an insufficient staff budget for larger student bodies.

The overall average of cost for instruction per student in the thirty-four schools does not reveal the significant fact of wide variations between the individual schools—from seven schools with an instruction expense per student varying from $122 to $200 to four schools whose expenses for instruction per student range from $600 to $770.

One other comparison is important in evaluating the professional character of library schools: the funds made available by the institutions for research. In the eight universities the library schools were next to the lowest of the nine different types of professional school in amount of research funds available during the year 1948–49. In fact, only $4,320 was available during that year in all eight library schools of the sample, compared with more than $1,000,000 for engineering, much more than $100,000 each for business and for education,

[5]Committee on the Economic Status of the Profession, American Association of University Professors, *op. cit.*, pp. 778–797.

about $15,000 each for architecture and law, $8,600 for journalism, and $6,500 for nursing. Only social work received less for this purpose.

If we compare the library schools, not with each other or with other professional schools, but with their own past, the showing is most hopeful. The present library schools are small, too small in many cases to be economical in operation or to assemble adequate teaching personnel, but they were smaller and fewer thirty years ago. The salaries, academic rank, teaching loads, provisions for retirement, leave, even funds for research have been growing steadily since then. The improvement, it is safe to assume, is owing largely to the movement which began at that time to include library schools as integral parts of colleges and universities, resulting in library school faculty members' sharing the benefits of salary scales and other regulations governing the teaching staffs generally in academic institutions.

In the academic hierarchy, library school faculties, teaching, and resources are in a position below, but not far below, the average, at least for schools of similar size. The findings of the Inquiry revealed more than anything else the great disparities between the individual library schools themselves. Some of these differences, perhaps most of them, reflect the differing academic standards of the colleges and universities of which they are a part. General improvement in library school instruction, then, may require consolidation of facilities in strong institutions rather than the attempt to improve the teaching resources and status of all existing schools by setting standards which some of the small and weak institutions cannot hope to meet.

LIBRARY SCHOOL PROGRAMS   As was pointed out earlier, the degree structure and curriculum of the accredited library schools were in transition during the years of the Public

Library Inquiry. The traditional programs away from which the schools were moving were evident enough. But the general nature of the modifications being made or proposed could be discerned only as tendencies rather than as definite new patterns.

From early in the century, when instruction in a long miscellany of useful library techniques came to be organized as orthodox academic courses, the subjects of study in library schools have consisted of four or five general required subjects and a greater number of elective and more specialized courses. The general subjects have been: (1) cataloguing and classification; (2) bibliography and reference; (3) book selection; (4) library administration; (5) history of libraries, books, and printing. The elective courses have dealt with the different types of institutions such as children's libraries, school libraries, college libraries, public libraries, music libraries, hospital libraries, special libraries in general, or have been devoted to special library techniques such as advanced cataloguing, reference, and classification. This has been the general course framework whether the library training unit is on the graduate or undergraduate level. Where the time allotted to the whole program was less than a year, as in the teachers' colleges training school librarians, the course in history of libraries, books, and printing has usually been dropped and the work in book selection and library administration has been oriented to children's literature and school library organization. But with these modifications the five general subject matters have constituted the core of the library school curriculum.

In the revised library school programs the traditional core seems to survive in every library school catalogue. Often there are different titles for the traditional content; there are changes in emphasis and in amount of time devoted to particular subjects. In line with the general purpose of giving the new programs a graduate-professional character suitable for acceptance by university authorities for the award of the master's rather than the bachelor's degree, some simpler techniques have been dropped out of required courses. This has been done especially in the courses in cataloguing, classification, bibliography and reference, where new emphasis is placed on the principles and theory inhering in these subjects.

In line with the same purpose of increasing the graduate-professional character of instruction, in most of the new programs book selection has been greatly enlarged so that it constitutes an evaluative survey of the literature of the three or four major fields of knowledge. In some schools book selection has become not one required course but several parallel courses included in the year's program. When combined with bibliography and reference, the expanded instruction in book knowledge has been erected into a central position in professional library education.

In some of the newer programs an attempt has been made to draw into one general course in library administration the essential material formerly in several elective courses dealing with the organization and the operating problems of the several types of libraries.

In more cases there is a modification of the course dealing with the general orientation of librarians hitherto presented in the form of an historical survey of library, books, and printing. In the development of library school curricula this course appeared later than the others, often remained an elective, and, as we have noted, has not been included in the curricula of the unaccredited library training centers for school librarians. In the expressed judgment of the large sample of librarians replying to the Inquiry questionnaire, moreover, history of books and libraries was the course of least value to them in their professional work. In the new programs, therefore, it is not surprising to see it relegated to an elective rather than a required status. In its place there have appeared courses under various titles (such as communication, libraries and the community, and so forth) that attempt to orient libraries and books largely in contemporary rather than historical terms. The new courses often include historical development along with contemporary analysis, but they draw mainly upon sociological method and literature.

These are the major modifications in the group of traditionally required courses. The courses now and formerly offered as electives do not form any consistent or new pattern in the new library school programs. Perhaps the most frequent addition or expansion here is in the field of reader guidance and adult education. A number of the new programs, using different course titles and arrangements of subject matter, seem to make increased use of psychology and pedagogy to interpret and adapt library materials to adults. These intellectual disciplines have previously been used mainly in relation to library work with children.

The increased amount of subject matter in the required courses of the new curricula has raised serious problems with regard to a place for specialized courses training students for particular types of libraries and of library work. It will be recalled that Williamson proposed that one entire year of the two years of professional instruction be devoted to this more specialized training; and in the traditional curricula such courses took most of the students' time in their second semester. The newer programs have in some cases greatly reduced the time for these electives in special libraries or special fields, but in practically all they still appear as part of the year's program. The most difficult library specialty to fit in as a part of a single year's general program is training for library work with children and in schools. In many, if not most, of the accredited library schools the solution has been to make an exception here by creating an alternative general program for children's librarians and school librarians, modifying the general program so that it includes the material needed in these two fields.

Another way of dealing with the general dilemma caused by expanding the content of the library school is to lengthen the period of total instruction beyond the established academic year of two semesters or three quarters. Some schools have required a fourth quarter or summer session in their new programs. A few others have defined some of the simpler library techniques as prerequisites for admission to the graduate-professional year, to be tested by examination before entrance. Still others have organized a total program which includes a semester or two quarters of library training on the undergraduate level combined with work for the general bachelor's degree. This is followed by the full academic year of post-bachelor work leading to the master's degree in librarianship. The undergraduate work is set up as a prerequisite for admission to the graduate-professional year. Considered alone, the undergraduate training entitles the student combining it with work for the bachelor's degree to be called a "subprofessional" librarian.

This curriculum development has led to definite disagreement among the library school innovators, most of whom are united on the changes in the curriculum to establish a clear basis for recognition of the year's work as of an advanced intellectual character properly leading to a master's professional degree. The device of moving the simpler library techniques down into the undergraduate years and making them a prerequisite for entrance to the graduate-professional library school is held by some library leaders to be a move directly opposite to the general objective. They argue that such a prerequisite handicaps excellent graduates of liberal arts colleges of high standing where the "subprofessional" techniques are not taught, making it difficult for them to gain entrance to the graduate library schools, and that these graduates are some of the best raw material of professional librarianship. Further-more, they argue that turning out bachelors of arts with a professional certificate, even if "sub-" is prefixed to it, will tend to blur the line between professional and nonprofessional positions in libraries and confuse still further the general pub-lic as to whether librarianship is an intellectual profession re-quiring prolonged training or a simple set of techniques to be picked up as part of a general education

The proponents of the two-step procedure in library train-ing, on the other hand, justify it as a means of establishing the truly advanced character of the year of graduate-professional training by keeping out of it the simpler techniques altogether. They urge, also, that the subprofessionals help to meet the acute current need for public librarians with as much training as possible in the small places that cannot afford to pay salaries which justify the prolonged training of the post-bachelor year. The disagreement reflects differences in the general academic programs and policies of universities and colleges in different parts of the country. It is not likely to be resolved easily. The library schools, in their replies to the Inquiry questionnaires, indicated no consensus on the subject.

Although the new library school programs are concentrated on providing the most suitable content for instruction leading to the basic professional degree, some attention is given in them also to the library school as a center for inquiry and ad-vanced instruction beyond the single post-bachelor year. That education on the graduate level involves training in methods of research or disciplined investigation is recognized in a num-ber of the schools where courses on research method and a master's thesis have been introduced. In at least one school, however, a field project has been substituted for the master's thesis that was formerly required in the two-year master's program; it was not clear which tendency is likely to prevail in the new programs, that is, the formal thesis with an empha-

sis on theory and method or the field project designed to
provide first-hand contact between the students and the types
of library and the kinds of problem which they will meet
in their daily work after graduation.

We have noted earlier that despite the proposal for a year
of internship in the influential Williamson report, this feature
of training used successfully for some of the older professions
has never taken hold in the library field. In the earlier library
training units the students were either in service in the library
where the school was located or did practice work in the
library during their training period. As theoretical background subject matter has replaced the simpler techniques,
the apprenticeship character of the year's work has been reduced. The Inquiry's survey of current practice showed that
laboratory work and group observation still constitute part
of the year's activity in a majority of the library schools. But
they seldom occupy more than the time of a single semester
course. One probable reason for the decline was evident from
the Inquiry questionnaires. They showed that at least three
fourths of the students who come to library schools have
already worked in libraries on a full-time, paid basis. And of
the students in library school 30 percent also hold library jobs
and are pursuing their professional education on a part-time
basis. Most, though not all, library school students, therefore,
are persons with some actual experience in libraries. This fact,
along with the limitation of formal training to one year probably explains the failure to require a more thoroughly organized period of laboratory work or internship as a requirement
for the granting of the basic professional library degree.

Another development in connection with the new school
programs has been the introduction of work leading to the
doctor's degree in three of the schools that formerly offered
the two-year master's degree. These are in addition to the
University of Chicago, which until now has been the only

institution serving as a center of research and instruction in librarianship beyond the master's level. In the public library field there has been little demand for the advanced research degree, and it is not clear that as yet the three new centers of advanced instruction will assume the obligation for encouraging and supporting faculty and advanced student research implied in offering the doctorate. In one of these programs, however (at Illinois), there is an attempt to combine student field observation and analysis with facilities for continuing research and experiment in library processes and services by making arrangements for the local public library to serve as a library laboratory for the graduate library school. It may be by this means that laboratory facilities and experience can be reintroduced into library training.

In still another direction the library schools recently have been assuming a function outside the traditional task of educating students for the basic professional degree. This has been the development of workshops, institutes, and conferences at the school for the intensive training of professional librarians in newer and more advanced phases of librarianship. Not many of the workshops have met for a long enough period to gain the full advantages of bringing together a group of skilled leaders to pursue the joint study of problems which concern them in their daily work. Not all of the workshops are on advanced levels. But the returns from the Inquiry questionnaires indicate a rapid, recent increase in workshops of all kinds, from six reported by all the schools in 1945 to thirty in 1948. Especially prominent were institutes or workshops concerned with problems presented in handling films and other non-book materials, personnel problems, problems of plant and equipment, and administrative problems in general.

In giving this review of the major features of the newer programs now in their first years, we have been tempted to assume the existence of a common pattern more than is warranted by a careful recording of the individual programs in each of the thirty-four schools. At present the schools are on their own, and it is difficult in some cases to see where they are going or whether they are moving at all except to change the letters symbolizing the professional degree. Two years ago the Board of Education for Librarianship, recognizing the major proportions of the changes being put into practice by several of the leading schools, withdrew temporarily from the task of accreditation. The resulting freedom has had salutary effects for experimentation. In the meantime, several new schools in universities of good standing have appeared. The feeling has grown recently that a comprehensive review of standards, programs, and degree structure is now due. Within the last few months the Board of Education for Librarianship has organized itself to conduct such a review. And it has associated with it for the purpose the Library Education Division of ALA, representing librarian opinion in general, and the Association of American Library Schools, the official agency of the accredited library schools themselves. What specific standards will emerge from this joint deliberation cannot be predicted. But it is safe to say that the result will be in the direction of establishing librarian training on a level appropriate for an organized intellectual profession. Here, as in the matter of economic status and occupational organization, the evidence indicates that the librarians have a long distance to go to gain full status and recognition as a profession. But the evidence indicates, also, that they are on their way.

II

THE DIRECTION OF DEVELOPMENT

WITH A GENERAL PICTURE of the present organization, resources, and services of the American public library now before us, we are in a position to suggest some of the concrete possibilities for library development during the decade ahead. If the development is to be sound, however, its direction will be defined by the public library objectives agreed upon in our opening chapters.

It will be recalled that the approach to public library objectives was by three routes. First was a review of library history to locate the librarian's traditional sense of purpose. Second was a synthesis of the statements of public library objectives promulgated in recent years by the official library leadership. This combined statement of current objectives was verified by submitting it to a representative sample of librarians and was found to reflect a consensus of librarian opinion. Third was a survey of the whole contemporary machinery of public communication of which the library is a part in order to see what role the public library might most appropriately play in the light of what is being done by other agencies.

The three routes converged upon each other in such a way as to establish the current, official formulation of library objectives firmly as the background against which to analyze present library organization and practice. In the current official statements of purpose the librarian's historic faith in the individual and social value of reading good books persists with undiminished vitality, but is enlarged so as to include other serious printed materials, pictures, films, and recordings. The functions currently claimed for public libraries by the librarians were found to be the very tasks which are left undone, or partially done, by the other communication agencies. And the neglected functions, under the assumptions accepted at the outset of the Inquiry, are important for the health of a democratic society. The survey of communication agencies underlined the librarian's emphasis on reliable material of cultural, educational, and informational value, calling attention to the inadequacy of commercial provision of materials outside the main stream of popular output, especially of critical, provocative, experimental products as well as the classic, standard enduring products of the past. The survey underlined, also, the indispensability of the library's function of not only assembling and preserving but also organizing and focusing for ready use materials of all kinds on particular subjects, problems, and interests.

With the interpretations and emphases given by the historical and sociological surveys, the official library objectives can serve most usefully as the basis for determining the direction of public library development. These objectives, most briefly paraphrased, are *to serve the community as a general center of reliable information and to provide opportunity and encouragement for people of all ages to educate themselves continuously.* And the functions for the public library agreed upon as the means of working toward the objectives are *to assemble, preserve, organize, and administer collections of books and other materials possessing cultural, educational, and informational value and to promote the public's use of library materials by active stimulation and skilled guidance.*

ALTERNATIVE DIRECTIONS   As was obvious from our canvass of librarian opinion, these definitions of objectives and functions are not accepted by all those presently in charge of public libraries. There was in our sample a small but energetic minority who see the public library's task solely as "giving people what they want," who would supply books, good or bad, on the basis of expressed public demand irrespective of quality, reliability, or value. To them public libraries are a free, miscellaneous book service supported by the public for that purpose rather than a governmental service of reliable information and continuous education as implied in the objectives approved by the majority of librarians.

This alternative objective not only turns away abruptly from the librarian's traditional faith in the ameliorative power of books, but also engages the public library in direct competition with the commercial agencies of communication on their own terms. As a long-term goal, it would assign to the public library a supplementary and secondary rather than distinctive role in the whole communication field, or would doom it to gradual extinction because of the greater resources, reach, and competitive skill of the commercial media of mass communication.

To have applied the alternative objective to present library practice and program would mean setting up the standards of mass production, distribution, and consumption as public library goals. To meet such standards would lead logically to central purchase of uniformly popular books and periodicals, and no others, to many small and large outlets dealing almost entirely with current publications manned by persons selected for qualities of salesmanship rather than scholarship, to results judged entirely in terms of volume of circulation and numbers of users. With such an objective the present organization, stock, and staff of public libraries would seem irrelevant or hopelessly inadequate. The current annual circulation averages of five or six per capita and 10 percent of adult users would constitute a confession of almost complete library failure. For these reasons, as well as the fact that this objective has only a minority of public librarians as adherents, it has not been used as a basis for assessing the present status of library development or the direction of its further development.

A second alternative concept of public library function and objective is at the other extreme from that of the librarians who reject the public library's educational purpose in favor of a miscellaneous free book service. This second minority, centering its attention on education as both objective and function, has moved away from the librarian's attachment to the handling of books and other materials as his special province. These librarians see the public library as a general agency of out-of-school education, with library materials as only one of its instruments.

In practice, the distinction between library functions as proposed by this minority group and as defined in the official majority statement is not as sharp as is indicated above. Indeed, the official statement of objectives may be interpreted very broadly to fit the minority's view. In performing the function of "active stimulation and skilled guidance," for instance, by use of lectures, forums, discussion groups or film showings, it is hard to draw the line between stimulation and guidance in thinking about important problems and stimulation and guidance in the use of books and films. The distinction is unreal and unimportant.

Nevertheless, the over-all difference between the public library performing a general function and performing a special function on behalf of out-of-school enlightenment is worth maintaining. It is the same difference that exists between the library of a university and the other university activities centered in classrooms and laboratories, all of which serve a common educational goal. We may extend the analogy by subsuming under the term "people's university" all the agencies of governmental, noncommercial, and serious commercial publication, university and school extension units, the numerous community clubs, societies, and other organizations whose activities have educational aspects, and the hosts of individual adults who are seeking reliable information, enlightenment, and inspiration. In line with the official definition of objectives the public library would be the library of such a people's university. As the general agency envisioned by the minority, it would itself constitute a people's university.

The idea of a tax-supported institution such as the public library assuming the character of a general agency of out-of-school education is logically sound. There may be particular places and occasions when a local library will assume the broader role successfully. But a pragmatic judgment based upon field observation and studies of the other adult education agencies in action in American states, cities, and rural localities, compared with present public library structure, resources, personnel, and political potential, and upon knowledge of the library's traditional faith in the virtue of books, led us to exclude this second alternative objective as a basis for assessing present public library achievement or charting the course of its proximate future. To have adopted the alternative would have assumed the existence of a purpose which few librarians have embraced and for attainment of which there would be required an almost revolutionary increase in available library funds, facilities, length, and breadth of professional training.

The suggestions of direction for public library development resulting from the Inquiry findings with regard to present library practice, then, are set within the framework of the current statement of official public library objectives and functions.

LARGER UNITS AND ADEQUATE FINANCIAL SUPPORT   A major direction for public library development in the decade ahead, in line with the official objectives, is the organization of larger public library systems and concentration of state and Federal financial aid on the encouragement and partial support of such systems. We have seen that public libraries in the United States have been organized as municipal services, that they are dependent on local initiative for their creation and on local tax sources for their support. The result is that half of the incorporated places are too small or too poor to have any public library, and two thirds of the people in the unincorporated areas are equally without direct library service. Furthermore, although there is a great multiplicity of independent library units, all but a tenth of them are so small or so poor that they cannot by themselves assemble a large enough stock of books and other materials or support the trained personnel to constitute a modern public library service as defined by the official objectives.

The emphasis in public library organization thus far has been on local initiative, citizen participation, adaptation of the service to the variant interests and conditions of different communities. There has been little attempt to gain the inherent economies and efficiencies of larger units in technical operations and in use of skilled personnel or by centralization to reduce the inequalities of service resulting from uneven distribution of population and economic resources. It is one of the assumptions of the Inquiry that in a large-scale modern democratic, industrial society there are advantages both in local initiative and participation and in larger units of administration; that neither should be neglected, but that governmental structure should be contrived to give the greatest possible scope to both principles.

The programs for larger library units and more adequate financial support being developed in several states seem designed to achieve this reconciliation. In practically all of them effort is made to pool the facilities of the existing public libraries within areas large enough: (*a*) to provide an adequate supply of books and other materials, (b) to enable the whole area to support a specialized professional staff, and (c) to use a headquarters technical staff to gain the economies of centralized ordering and processing of materials. In some states the existing public libraries of a populous county or region are consolidated into a library system for the whole region, with new outlets provided for localities hitherto without libraries. There is a single budget and administrative control, but local autonomy and citizen participation in the community outlets are maintained as far as possible. In other states existing libraries in an area of adequate size are federated to create for the whole region a pooled stock of materials and of professional personnel and to provide centralized processing, the constituent libraries retaining full autonomy in other respects. In still other states the state itself sets up and maintains in a region of its own making an auxiliary library service center and invites the libraries within the region to participate in a common book pool, in centralized ordering and processing, and in the use of a specialized, central staff for guidance and help. Under this arrangement the local libraries retain full self-government. The studies conducted by the Public Library Inquiry indicate that at present price levels at least $100,000 annual expenditures for the whole library system, including pooled stocks and personnel in the co-operating libraries, is required for maintaining a regional library with resources sufficient to provide modern public library service.

In the federated system and the state auxiliary regional library unit it would be possible, by the pooling of staff, stock, processes, and services, to include some of or all the facilities of the school, college, and university libraries of the region. The latter libraries, it should be noted, share the structural characteristics of public libraries in the United States in that they consist of a multiplicity of independent units—many of them very small.

The movement for building larger public library systems by consolidation, federation, or voluntary association has centered attention largely on less populous areas. It is equally desirable as a direction for development, however, in metropolitan regions. As we have seen, public library systems which cover the whole of a metropolitan area exist almost nowhere in the United States. The organization of libraries under municipal corporations here, as in less populous areas, militates against complete coverage of the area, and voluntary cooperation to provide an integrated service for the whole metropolis has seldom been carried out. But a pooling of resources in large urban areas has as much promise of economy as in rural regions.

Larger library service units of themselves help to reduce the inequalities of service arising from inequalities of tax resources between localities. But, as we have noted, local sources of taxation are so limited in most states that if public libraries are to approach the objectives of service laid down by their leaders there needs be some participation by the state in their financial support. State aid to public libraries hitherto has been so extremely small that it has scarcely affected either the quality or quantity of library service for the country as a whole. The direction of desirable development has been given in a few states, however, by voting state grants in substantial amounts, but limiting them to city, county, or regional library systems large enough to do the modern library job. In this way state participation in support of the public libraries not only provides much-needed supplementary revenue but also accelerates the reorganization of the library systems themselves, whether in rural regions or in metropolitan urban centers, to take full advantage of the economies and greater resources inherent in larger units.

The impetus to adequate laws for larger library units and for state money grants to aid such units will necessarily depend upon the professional and lay library organizations and state library officials. The administration of laws, regulations, standards, state aid, Federal grants if made, and auxiliary regional library centers will fall to the state library officers and staff. Library development in line with the official goals, therefore, will mainly depend in the next ten years on building large, inclusive, professional library associations in each state, in mobilizing trustees and other lay groups for support of the statewide programs, and in building competent, professional leadership, official sponsorship, and an expert staff in the state library itself.

Federal grants of modest amounts in aid of specified state programs for building larger library units in areas where they do not exist would also be in the direction of development indicated above as desirable. If the Federal funds are not to be wasted in some of the states having grossly inadequate state library staffs and funds, the creation of an adequate state library unit must be a condition for the grant. With such a provision Federal grants in the next decade would serve to stimulate the development of a modern public library program, especially in the laggard states, without removing the major responsibility for public library direction and support from the states and localities.

A more fundamental type of Federal participation in public library development in the years ahead is by leadership and financial support of the country's research library and bibliographic facilities. Co-operative planning among the great research libraries is already under way in some areas. There are allocations for current purchases, regional bibliographic centers, regional storage centers, plans for centralization and allocation of bibliographical services. The plans and programs are essentially interstate or national in character. They are thus peculiarly appropriate subjects for Federal rather than state or local financial support. Furthermore, Federal grants would be likely to supply the necessary impetus to carry through voluntary co-operative agreements between the country's research libraries. A network of agreements and regional centers for inter-library loans and storage thus brought into being would constitute a highly useful public librarian's library. Just as intra-state regional library systems make the materials resources of the region's library available to the library patron in any one of its localities, so a national research library network provided with Federal funds for interlibrary services would make the country's specialized and scholarly materials in original or duplicated form available to the qualified users of any of the nation's public libraries.

MATERIALS AND SERVICES   The development of public libraries in accordance with the official objectives calls for an increase of materials and expansion of services. The Inquiry's sampling of holdings and current purchases revealed that small public libraries—which means two thirds of them—tend to buy and hold collections of popular current fiction more than anything else and that these small libraries make no serious attempt, by building stocks of popular but authoritative reference works to "serve the community as a general center of reliable information." The sampling showed that with few exceptions adequate periodical collections including bound volumes existed in only the 6 percent of the nation's public libraries which have budgets of $25,000 or more. It indicated, further, that stocks of nontheatrical films and of music materials, including recordings, are limited largely to the even smaller percentage of public libraries with budgets of $100,-000 or more. Government publications suitable for popular use, which are not expensive, but are harder to select and order than best sellers, appear in quantity only in these larger public libraries. Thus the traditional system of small, independent public library units has resulted in severe limitations on the quantity, quality, and variety of materials available for circulation and reference in most localities.

As long as the libraries remain small and isolated from each other these limitations are inevitable. The development of more adequate materials and services, thus, depends on the prior development of larger units of service aided by substantial increases of financial support. With larger systems and increased funds, pooled collections of books, periodicals, and government documents of large size can replace separate small stocks; by a system of scheduled circulation large collections of films and records can be made available to all the localities in a region; a headquarters reference unit and professional expert advisers on children's reading programs and materials suitable for other groups can serve all localities, large and small, within the area. The library patrons in tiny villages and on farms can have direct access to the wealth of modern library materials and professional services now available only in the larger and better city library systems.

Fundamental public library service will continue to be based on large and varied collections of materials available generally for individual borrowers and reference workers. But in their positive role of "stimulating" and "furnishing expert guidance" in the use of materials public libraries are increasingly providing special collections, programs, and other services under professional direction for serious groups in the community with special problems and interests. Musicians, writers, women's clubs, business and labor organizations, government administrative and legislative officials are among those frequently given special attention and help. The librarians in these tasks bring to full focus their unique skills for the benefit of important segments of the community.

Group services constitute a direction for public library activity which may wisely be expanded as funds and personnel make it possible.

As yet the public library has not been widely used as the official materials and program center for more formally-organized adult education groups under the auspices of public schools, universities, and agricultural extension agencies. In many places, especially as larger library systems are organized, the public library would appear to be well suited to provide the materials and sometimes the meeting centers which these formal educational enterprises require. Direct functioning in connection with such adult education enterprises would be an expansion of public library activity in line with the accepted library objectives.

One of the oldest and most successful library services to identified groups is work with children and young people. It is today the major public library activity in terms of patronage and widely recognized librarian skill for all but the very large city libraries. With the emergence of school libraries in recent years, the public library is necessarily involved in restudying its service for these groups. For the next decade, at least, neither the public library nor the school library is equipped or operated so as to perform the whole function itself. The situation calls for a positive program of co-operation on all levels between the two agencies. The form of co-operation will vary in different localities. But on the public librarian's part it requires full and sympathetic understanding of the increasing function and importance of the school library in modern public education. A desirable step toward common understanding and planning would be to make the professional training of school, children's, and young people's librarians identical and the posts in school and public libraries interchangeable. The latter change would also require action by public library administrators to equate the salaries, hours of work, and vacations of children's and young people's librarians with similar positions in the school libraries. The disadvantage in these matters under which public libraries labor in recruiting and keeping children's librarians presents an acute, immediate problem in maintaining children's work in the public libraries.

The development of materials and services in public libraries does not depend entirely on adequate sizes of units and sufficient funds. There are alternative directions in which any public library, large or small, rich or poor, can move, depending on the concept of function held by its librarian, library staff, and library board. To what extent shall the librarian select materials for their quality and reliability? How much shall he concentrate on seeking out and serving groups limited in size, but serious in their interests? How far shall he resist the pressures of groups in the community, or of one or more of his own trustees, to exclude from his collection serious, significant, but unpopular or unorthodox, materials? How much in new purchases shall he yield to the best-seller selections created by high-powered commercial advertising?

As far as the statements of official objectives are concerned, especially when interpreted against the background of the whole business of communication, the direction of public library policy seems clear. Its distinctive function is to emphasize quality and reliability in current purchases rather than popularity as such; to make available the less accessible materials for serious groups in the community, however small; to keep open a broad highway of free access to the more daring, more provocative, often unpopular current ideas, proposals, and criticisms, as well as the more generally approved materials.

But actual progress in this direction is not easy. It is one of the assumptions of the Inquiry that here lie points of inevitable tension in public library administration, as in the administration of other social agencies. There are individual and social values of primary importance in making new ideas, insights, and free critical expression as widely available as possible through the agencies of public communication. But in the freest societies there are some prohibitions on pictures and print on behalf of safety, decency, and morality. The librarian, therefore, is bound to make difficult judgments of public concern in his selection and rejection of materials. In his selection of material for reliability and quality, also, he is involved in the almost inevitable tension arising from the differences between his professional judgments as a librarian and the opinions and preferences of the lay members of the community.

In both areas of tension actual practice is likely to be a compromise. A library may decide to provide an extended service of current best sellers on a self-supporting rental basis along with current materials selected for quality and reliability available on free loan. It may enter upon a policy of gradual reduction of trashy current material on a long-term basis. It may provide only limited access to unorthodox publications. The important matter to be kept in mind is that the director and staff know what they are doing and in what direction they are going. The rate of progress toward the attainment of the official objectives will, by necessity, vary from place to place.

ORGANIZATION AND MANAGEMENT   If in the years ahead public libraries are to become larger, more complex operating units, with financial support coming from both the localities and the state, increased attention must be given to executive-policy direction and to internal administrative management. In both these matters the Inquiry studies found great differences in effectiveness among libraries.

With regard to top policy and political leadership what

seemed most needed was clarification of the proper roles of the librarian and the library board rather than changes in the legal structure of the boards or the method of their appointment. Although the Inquiry examined public libraries operating successfully without any board at all, it seemed evident that for the next decade the appointed board of trustees or directors will be the prevailing form for lay control of the public library. If the board's role were clearly defined as a group to provide seasoned lay judgments on the library's general policy and program (including judgment on the continuing effectiveness of the chief librarian) and to furnish active sponsorship of the program and budget before the general government and community, the obvious weaknesses presently existing in board personnel and procedures might be greatly reduced. Appointments to the board would be made more frequently with an eye especially to seasoned judgment, civic spirit, and broadly representative quality and prestige as qualifications for appointment and reappointment. Formal rules or customs of tenure would tend to develop to assure continued vigor and new points of view in the board's chairmanship and membership. Board procedures would be so arranged that the time at meetings would more regularly be devoted to policy and strategy rather than to administrative detail as is now too often the case. Similarly, if the chief librarian's role were clearly defined as including the political and policy, as well as administrative, aspects of executive leadership it might be expected that more and more often persons having the required qualifications would be chosen for that post.

Individual board sponsorship and librarian leadership will need to be supplemented on both local and state levels in order to secure adequate financial support for the public library's enlarged program. Well-organized local and state associations of librarians working in close relation to organized groups of local board members and active and appreciative library users are indicated as the most effective means of translating knowledge of and enthusiasm for effective library service into persuasion of the officers of the general government to approve a modern public library program and the funds to support it.

Equal attention should be paid to the administrative management of public libraries. The Inquiry studies indicated that the greatest possibilities for improvement in the years ahead depend not so much upon analysis of internal formal structure as of flow of work, definition of duties, disposition of personnel, and simplification of processes. Here, as in the development of more adequate materials and services, management and personnel analyses await the emergence of larger public library units. The great number of small public libraries, because of their size, are inherently inefficient in their conduct of work and organization of personnel. But as the public library units become larger, especially as more systems appear with small units serving as parts of or in co-operation with a large unit, there is definitely an opportunity to increase efficiency by using the specialized skills of management analysis and of personnel specialists.

For each library system, whether municipal, regional, or state, this involves the inclusion in top staff positions of experts in charge of management studies and of experts in personnel administration. It will require also the spread among professional librarians generally of an understanding of the importance of these special skills. And it will mean the incorporation of both a scientific personnel program and an operations-analysis program into the library's regular administrative system.

Especially for the small units within a larger system there is opportunity through expert guidance to simplify and to rationalize the small units' daily operations, to simplify procedures, and to establish standards of work accomplishment of value for comparative studies of the units within the system. Eventually there will be opportunity for larger comparisons between two or more homogeneous library systems themselves. Similarly, there will be gains from the development of common job definitions, salary grades, and other personnel procedures of an orderly nature within the parts of a single library system and between systems in a state or a region.

The introduction of these expert techniques of management presents subtle problems of adaptation. It is one of the assumptions of the Inquiry that librarians, like other professional groups, are sensitive with regard to the values of their traditional ways and will be slow to accept changes in accustomed practices recommended by outside specialists. It is also assumed that some changes would be desirable. It is, therefore, of great importance that the skills of management analysis and scientific personnel administration be assimilated within the general administration of libraries and professional training of librarians rather than occasionally presented as an intrusion of outsiders to measure work, to analyze and classify positions, or to establish salary grades.

PERSONNEL   A public library personnel adequate for the accomplishment of the official public library objectives depends fully as much on the organization of larger library systems as do adequate materials, services, and management economies. With the emergence of larger units, however, the group of positions in public libraries for which professional training is required, can be identified and persons can be educated to fill them. The direction of library personnel development in line with the objectives in the years ahead would seem to be toward a more highly trained and a more highly organized professional group.

There are at least four main elements in such a program.

First is scientific job analysis and job classification to define the professional and other positions in each library, already referred to as a function of modern library management. Second is a general system of certification of librarians who have the professional training and experience to qualify them for the professional positions. Certification may be based primarily on examinations given by professional or by civil service authorities, or it may be based on a professional degree from a library school accredited by a professional agency as having adequate resources, standards, and programs for professional training. A combination of the two may develop by which the degree from an accredited school is accepted in lieu of an assembled written examination, required of those whose professional training has been obtained outside accredited schools. Third is the organization of a satisfactory professional career in public libraries. This means the maintenance of a general salary level on an equality with other occupations with similar types of work and length of training (that is, teaching and social work), and of regular, graded salary increases equivalent to importance of work, and opportunity for promotion to the top positions without discrimination. It means also the organization of general machinery for security provisions for illness, accidents, and old age, especially needed in an occupation with very modest salary rewards, the regulation of leaves of absence and vacations, and the participation in policy deliberations appropriate for a professionally conscious group.

THE LIBRARY SCHOOLS   An adequate supply of professional librarians competent to carry on the enlarged public library tasks in the years ahead will depend to a large degree on the quality of the library schools. The studies of the Inquiry indicated that many of the "accredited" library schools are too small, too poor in budgetary and faculty resources and equipment to provide the instruction, research, and leadership called for if public libraries are to move significantly toward their accepted objectives.

The program of library school development indicated by the objectives seems to be a full year of basic professional education beyond the bachelor's degree and consolidation of such professional training as far as possible in library schools, with the faculty and other resources available only in universities with high academic standards and well-developed graduate and professional schools. It is difficult to say whether this consolidation of school facilities will be achieved by a revised system of accreditation under the Board of Education for Librarianship or by the slower process of growth by grants and other professional recognition of a dozen or more strong regional schools with the quality and prestige to attract most of the promising students and to furnish the recruits for most of the better jobs. The other professions illustrate both lines of development.

Insofar as the programs of the library schools are directed toward the official objectives they are likely to increase the time and attention given to the background knowledge for book selection, reference, reader guidance, and analysis of the setting of public library service in the contemporary community and in the whole field of communication of which the library is a part. There is likely, also, to be more attention to the backgrounds in scientific political studies, personnel administration, and management analysis, valuable for public library organization and administration. In the university library schools, with the co-operation of schools of education, the training of children's and school librarians is likely to be unified in one curriculum.

The dilemma of the need for more subject matter in professional education and the limitation of the period of training to the one post-bachelor year is likely to lead in the stronger schools to an increase in the number of workshops or institutes devoted to special subjects designed for the short-term, advanced training of librarians now in service. And the need to verify the direction and rate of change in library procedures will be served by increasing the provision for sustained mature research and laboratory study of public library problems in the three or four library schools offering advanced instruction for the research degree as well as others having the requisite personnel and facilities.

With the emergence of larger public library systems and the clear demarcation of the professional positions in the libraries, there will be an increasing proportion of nonprofessional, technical jobs for which training is required. Although some of this training may be offered in academic institutions, it would seem desirable to distinguish sharply between instruction for nonprofessional technical jobs, whether in service or in school, and the graduate instruction for the professional degree and title of librarian, as outlined above.

IN THE YEARS AHEAD   Each of the special studies of the Public Library Inquiry has analyzed a particular aspect of the library system in the United States. Through them we have been able to discern specific problems and to suggest desirable directions of library development. But what will public libraries as a whole look like ten years from now if librarians work actively toward the objectives upon which they are officially agreed?

It is in the nature of social science inquiry to emphasize analysis of present and past institutional structure and performance, but to be cautious about predicting the shape of things to come. Workers in the library vineyard, therefore, must look elsewhere for those pictures of library utopias which, although they may provide a much needed inspiration for the day's work, are not constructed out of actual probabilities, trends, and achievements. Nevertheless, it is possible to stay within the bounds of possibility tempered with optimism and to put together out of trends and instances a picture of what public libraries might be if in 1960 most libraries shall have arrived at the point where a small number are now. We must attach the additional proviso also that during this period libraries do not suffer from the drastic diversion of public resources and energies necessitated by a major war or depression.

Within such limitations we might look forward to a yearly expenditure 50 percent larger than the hundred million dollars spent in the last year in the United States for public library operation. With this money and assuming a reorganization of structure and personnel a greatly improved library service could come into being.

We might have less than a thousand public library systems, which together would serve the whole population. Some would be the familiar city systems having a headquarters library and a number of branches. But by extension, contract, or other co-operative arrangement, a city system would serve the whole metropolitan region of which it is the center. Outside the cities the large numbers of small and middle-size libraries would continue to serve the communities which created them. But they would be related to other libraries in groups to constitute regional library systems with general pools of books and other materials, with specialized professional personnel available for guidance throughout the system, with a centralized system of reference and for processing of books and materials, usually located in the largest library within the system.

Each library within the system would have its own appointed librarian and library board, could order its own books, and could carry on its own distinctive library services. But in addition, its patrons might through it have access to a pooled book collection totaling at least 100,000 volumes, renewed annually by current purchases of all the books of value in each year's published output, to a central reference collection equivalent to a large city headquarters library, to a collection of music records, scores, and books, and to films circulated through libraries in the system to groups in each community. Within the regional library system a specialist in children's literature would be making her rounds of the communities, providing story hours, talks to parents, and guidance to librarians in the choice and handling of children's books. Similarly, a specialist in work with adults would be in the field, advising adult groups and stimulating the use of books, films, records, pamphlets, and government documents throughout the region. From headquarters, also, a specialist in technical processes and management analysis would be available to help small local librarians without professional training to perform their work more economically and expeditiously. Each day, in response to telephone calls or written requests, trucks and cars would carry books, information, and library personnel back and forth between the headquarters and the community libraries. The card in any library of the region would be a regional card so that any card holder could visit other libraries, including the headquarters library, to borrow or to return books or other materials. The headquarters catalogues would list and locate all the books within the region. In short, with allowances for more time in communication and transport, the regional libraries would provide the wealth of materials and services now available only in better city library systems.

Alongside the public library system, insofar as school authorities accept the objectives of general library development proposed by public library leaders and finance that development, there might be a system of school libraries, professionally manned, in all high schools and in all but the smaller elementary schools. In the school libraries there would be the reading and audio-visual materials needed in the school's instruction, including supplementary materials that enrich the work of the classroom. School libraries, like public libraries, would benefit by pooling and circulating books and other materials, central processing, and professional guidance. In most communities, during the next ten years at least, the community public library facilities would also be needed for the work of high school students because of their availability in the evening and during vacations and because some valuable public library materials are not in the school collections. This use of the public library by high school students would, by co-operation between school and library personnel, be made the natural means of introduction to the adult services of the public library.

For the elementary and pre-school children, there could be a variety of ways by which children's and school library services would be correlated. In some places, especially in rural areas, the public library's children's department would provide and staff elementary school library service. In others it would supplement the school library with more varied collections and services available outside of school hours and terms and by materials for parents of preschool children. In such cases joint selection and processing for the two pooled collections might be maintained. But in any case the school would accept full financial responsibility for financing the library services in the schools, and the public library would promote an increase in the number and quality of separately-manned school libraries.

A third network, that of the research library services, could be developed to provide economies in assembling and preserving the scarcer library materials and machinery to make these materials generally available to public and college libraries by loan or by photographic reproduction. With central co-ordination and financial aid provided through the Library of Congress, there might be a score or more of inter-state area centers in or near the country's great research li-braries. These centers would aid in the economical storage of less-used but valuable materials, in the economical purchasing of new materials, and in providing machinery for location and interlibrary loans of all materials for serious use. The centers would serve each public, college, university, and special li-brary of the area; in co-operation they would all serve the libraries of the nation.

The three networks of library service, public, school, and research, when fully developed, would provide people of all ages in all places in the United States with abundant op-portunity to learn so far as library materials can give that op-portunity. This would mean that children in every town and village and school district would have available the wealth of modern and classic children's books and that their parents would be advised and stimulated in the guidance of their children's reading by librarians who know what children's literature is best adapted to all ages. It would mean that the woman's club chairman would receive skilled guidance and selected materials for her study program of the year and that the musicians of a town would have a library of music books, records, and scores no one of them could afford to own. It would mean that the serious, specialized worker living many miles from the nearest village would, via bookmobile, regional library, and area bibliographical center, have available to him the specialized literature of his field. Every adult seeking in-formation or reading for his own interests and needs would have recourse to a library and the services of a librarian to help him get what he wants. In the broadest sense, his library would be the library resources of the whole country.

The building of such a truly national library service would

cost money, but a tiny amount compared with the major
public services. More than money, librarians would be required with the imagination to see the possibilities of public
library services in their modern setting and the skill and co-
operative ability to bring them into being.

APPENDIX
METHODS AND SOURCES

IN THE FOREWORD AND FIRST CHAPTER of the present volume a description is given of the general framework within which the specific studies of the Inquiry were planned. The problem to be attacked was stated and its scope defined. The basic social goals and generalizations derived from examination of other social institutions which the Director and staff brought to the study of the public library were set down as explicit assumptions. The special character of the Inquiry as an independent analysis of the public library institution by persons representing, not one, but several social science disciplines was emphasized.

A word of explanation needs to be added concerning the Inquiry's relation to social science research and to practical public library planning. As to general method, the Inquiry falls definitely into the category of social engineering or applied rather than pure social science research. It was suggested in the Foreword that engaging specialists from the various social science disciplines to apply their distinctive methods of analysis to a single social institution with an orchestration of findings into a unified general report might have methodological significance beyond the major purposes of the study. Those engaged in the Inquiry have hoped also that the content of the findings themselves would add their mite to the whole body of reliable knowledge regarding contemporary American social institutions. This is all to the good. But refinement of the methods of social research or adding small segments of verified facts to the general stream of scientific data in circumscribed fields constitutes incidental by-products rather than central objectives of this particular type of investigation. The Inquiry's major purpose was rather to bring together a foundation of reliable knowledge and objective interpretation for policy making and action by those who operate or directly influence public libraries in the United States. Its assignment was comprehensive specific, its period of operation and funds were strictly limited. If its results were to be useful, they must be such that they could be taken hold of by librarians today in planning for the predictable future—estimated by the Inquiry to be, at most, the next ten years.

On the other hand, the Inquiry was not an official agency charged with the responsibility of promulgating a program to meet pressing public library problems or to provide any single right course of action for librarians. Its task was to organize existing data and to develop relevant new data on libraries, to bring to bear on the library as an institution generalizations derived from the analysis of other social institutions, of social forces and trends, and to evaluate the data for the use of those who play an active role in public library planning. Thus, although the Inquiry's function implied maintaining a vital connection with the specific circumstances, traditions, and outlook of the libraries of today, its value lay in providing background, breadth, and perspective for the decisions to be made in the present decade.

THE PROJECTS   This determination of the Inquiry's distinctive function explains the selection, range, and limitations of its special studies. Restriction of time, funds, available techniques, and personnel meant that certain fundamental studies of great value in appraising the public library's contribution to our society could not be undertaken with any hope that they would be available for use at the end of two and a half years—for example, studies of the actual effect of the services of the public library on people's lives and the activities of communities. So, also, the library's historic and present preoccupation with books indicated that no radical change in library functions which relegated books to a minor or secondary role would make any connection with present library realities.

Even more severe were the limitations imposed by the necessity of gaining in a short time a knowledge of the operating realities of an institution with more than 7,000 units varying in size and strength, located in forty-eight states, each of which possesses different library laws and social and economic character. The device of sampling, involving a purely practical balancing of the advantages of extensive coverage with intensity and depth of analysis of single units, was adopted. Results from such a technique could only be approximations. But they avoided the extremes of the thin and lifeless picture gained from extensive, statistical coverage and the distorted result of intensive analysis of only a few libraries selected for convenience or reputation.

The projects for study were selected on the basis of loosely defined hypotheses relating to lack of adaptation of public libraries to (a) important changes of the last decades in institutions and techniques of mass communication, (b) needs for civic enlightenment, (c) shifts in governmental structure, (d) means of financial support, and (e) occupational opportunities for women.[1]

The individual projects differed considerably in their use of specifically formulated hypotheses. The studies of public library personnel and of public library book and periodical holdings, for instance, used the strict null hypothesis form. Others, such as the study of library government, were more loosely organized, combining a preliminary period of exploration and case studies with gradually emerging hypotheses set for test and verification. A few, such as the Heindel memorandum on foreign library development and the Hardy study of public library evolution, were wholly exploratory in design and execution. This variety of project design reflected the interdisciplinary character of the Inquiry.

The nineteen projects, constituting the major work of the Inquiry, were divided into three types. A group of nine projects dealt directly with the major elements in the public library as an operating entity; its personnel, government, finance, materials, processes, and use, or clientele.

The study of public library personnel was conducted by Alice I. Bryan, assisted by Phyllis Osteen of the New York Public Library staff in the assembling of the literature of personnel grading and classification. A separate study of the professional

[1]These hypotheses are included in the first statement of the plan of the Inquiry published in the *Library Journal*, LXXII (May 1, 1947), 698, 720–724.

education of librarians which constitutes a section of the general project on library personnel was conducted by the Director. He was assisted by Lucy Crissey, of the staff of the School of Library Service of Columbia University, in collating the current library school programs. The results of these studies are brought together in one of the series of Inquiry reports to be published by the Columbia University Press under the title *The Public Librarian*.[2]

The study of public library government was in charge of Oliver Garceau. Associated with him as a team to carry on the field investigations were C. Dewitt Hardy, Lillian Orden, Watson O'D. Pierce, and the Director. Miss Orden also made a study of Federal library agencies and activities, which was presented as a draft memorandum for use in the Garceau project. And Mr. Hardy made a study of the evolution of the public library in America, which, in addition to serving the general purposes of the Inquiry as historical background, was summarized and included as the first chapter of the published volume by Oliver Garceau. This book, entitled *The Public Library in the Political Process*, presented the findings of the project on library government.

The study of public library book and periodical resources was conducted by the Director. The findings, summarized in Chapter 5 of the present volume, are to be presented more fully in an article to appear in *The Library Quarterly* in the fall of 1950.

The project on public library processes was carried on by Nejelski and Co., management consultants, under the supervision of Watson O'D. Pierce. The report of the project has been made available in mimeographed form under the title "Work Measurement in Public Libraries."

The study of public library finance was conducted by Charles Armstrong and is being made available in mimeographed form with the title "Money for Libraries."

A project on the use and users of the public library and other media of large-scale communication, carried on by intensive interviews of citizens constituting a national sample, was conducted

---

[2] See last page of the present volume for full list of the printed and mimeographed reports of the Inquiry.

for the Inquiry by the Michigan Survey Research Center under the general direction of Rensis Likert and the immediate supervision of Charles Metzner. The findings have been mimeographed as "The Public Library and the People."

A related project, consisting of a critical comparative analysis of all the more important studies of library use and users of the other media, including the Likert findings, was made by Bernard Berelson assisted by Lester Asheim of the faculty of the Graduate Library School of the University of Chicago. This study has been published under the title *The Library's Public*.

Separation of a single institution for special study is an act of artificial isolation. A full picture of the functions and trends of the public library was to be gained only by examining the institutions outside the library which serve it, influence it, or compete with it. The second group of six projects, therefore, had to do with peripheral agencies and activities.

A study of trade-book publishing and distribution was made by William Miller and has been published under the title *The Book Industry*. Mr. Miller also brought together the available literature analyzing the magazine industry, which was presented as an unpublished draft memorandum to the Director.

James L. McCamy, assisted by Julia McCamy, made a study of the publication and distribution of government documents which has been published under the title *Government Publications for the Citizen*.

In co-operation with the Twentieth Century Fund, Gloria Waldron, of the Fund's staff, conducted a study of the production and distribution of nontheatrical films. Cecile Starr, then of the staff of the American Association of Adult Education, assisted in this project by visits and questionnaires to libraries distributing these films. The study has been published under the title *The Information Film*.

An analysis of the music industry and music materials in relation to the public library was carried on by Otto Luening, assisted by H. R. Shawhan, of Columbia University. A draft memorandum was also prepared for Mr. Luening by Eloise Moore, of Bennington College, on the use and distribution of non-music recordings. The report of the study has been made available in mimeographed form under the title "Music Materials and the Public Library; an analysis of the role of the public library in the field of music."

In co-operation with the Bureau of Applied Social Research, Joseph Klapper made a critical analysis of existing researches dealing with effects on readers and audiences of the major media of mass communication. This study has been mimeographed as "The Effects of Mass Media."

The third group of four projects provided general background for the final report and for the Inquiry as a whole. They were submitted to the Director in the form of memoranda and have not been given separate publication. They are: (1) a study by the Director of the current statements of official public library objectives and verification of the extent of librarian acceptance of the objectives; (2) a general survey by Richard Heindel of recent foreign and international developments in the library field; (3) a survey of available literature with regard to special libraries by Helen Roberts; and (4) an analysis of the degree of civic information and interest possessed by people as judged by polls and voting percentages, also by Helen Roberts.

THE SAMPLE LIBRARIES   Various methods were employed in the nineteen projects. Several of them, however, used the sampling technique to obtain quantitative information. For their joint use a sample of sixty public libraries was constructed. The list was made up in two parts. The primary sample consisted of forty-seven libraries, located in forty-three cities, towns, and villages, and, in the case of seventeen communities, the adjoining rural areas. The designation of these particular places was made by the University of Michigan Survey Research Center, employing techniques developed and tested by the United States Department of Agriculture and other sampling agencies over a period of years. On the basis of five variables of population composition (urbanization, per capita war bond sales, percentage of wage earners in manufacturing industries, percentage of native whites, and average size of farm) all the counties in the United States outside the twelve largest metropolitan areas were classified into twenty-seven strata, or groups, each containing an equal proportion of the adult population. From each stratum one county was designated on a completely chance basis (use of random numbers) as representative of all the counties in the stratum. The twelve largest metropolitan areas were separately stratified, and the sample areas were designated by use of the same techniques as for the counties.

By these means a population cross-section representative of the country as a whole was constructed. The sample could be used to obtain an approximation of the quantity of library service rendered by the American people. By the further technique of random selection of citizens for individual interviews known as area sampling, it provided the Inquiry with a statistically-reliable description of citizen use of, non-use of, and attitudes toward the public library.

The dragnet of selection of public libraries by chance to secure a cross section of the population included libraries of various sizes and widespread geographical location. It did not, however, automatically include all types of public library organization or services. To provide this variety, thirteen other public library systems were chosen according to the pooled ratings of three library experts for superiority either in development of extended services or general level of service to the public. The combined list of sixty libraries included fifty municipal libraries serving communities ranging in size from 2,500 population to the largest metropolitan areas, and ten county library systems of almost equally diverse size and function.

The total sample did not provide a numerically accurate cross section of the 7,408 public library units in the United States which would be appropriate for statistical analysis of organization or services. It did, however, exemplify various types of library service available to diverse population groups in various geographical locations, and it provided a comprehensive range of library structure and experience satisfactory for quantitative surveys. The number of libraries in the sample appeared to be near the point where enlargement would have meant diminishing returns through duplication of very similar patterns of experience. It was a practical maximum considering the money and time available for staff visits.

The use of the same libraries by those conducting the poll of library users, study of library personnel, library government, library processes, books, documents, music, and film materials made possible economies in visits and interviews and provided a valuable cross check of staff observations and accumulated data. The explanations of the purpose of the various projects made by staff members in their visits also resulted in obtaining a maximum of co-operation on the part of the libraries in the sample.

LIBRARIES IN THE SAMPLE

CITY AND TOWN LIBRARIES

Aberdeen, Wash.
Baltimore, Md.
Bangor, Me.
Bethlehem, Pa.
Boston, Mass.
Bristol and Bucks County, Pa.**
Centralia and Marion County, Ill.**
Chattanooga and Hamilton County, Tenn.*
Chicago, Ill.
Cincinnati and Hamilton County, Ohio*
Cleveland, Ohio
Denver, Colo.
Detroit, Mich.
Evansville, Ind.
Flint, Mich.
Geneva and Geneva County, Ala.**
Greeley, Colo.
Huntingsburg, Ind.
Huntsville, Ala.

Jackson, Miss.
Jasper and Dubois County, Ind.**
Knoxville, Tenn.
Larchmont, N. Y.
Litchfield and Meeker County, Minn.*
Little Ferry, N. J.
Long Beach, Calif.
Lynn, Mass.
Montclair, N. J.
Mt. Vernon, Ind.
Newark, N. J.
New Orleans, La.
New York, N. Y.
Norwalk, Conn.
Perry and Noble County, Okla.*
Pine Bluff and Jefferson County, Ark.*
Racine, Wis.
Rochester, N. Y.
St. Louis, Mo.

San Francisco, Calif.
Scranton and Lackawanna
  County, Pa.**
Seattle, Wash.
Shelton, Conn.
Solvay, N. Y.
Springfield and Windsor
  County, Vt.*

Staunton and Augusta County,
  Va.*
Syracuse, N. Y.
Toledo, Ohio
University City, Mo.
Warren, Ohio
Wilmette, Ill.

SEPARATE COUNTY LIBRARIES

Genesee County, Mich.†
Grays Harbor County, Wash.†
Hinds County, Miss.†
Kern County, Calif.‡
King County, Wash.†

Lancaster County, S. C.‡
Lubbock County, Tex.‡
Portage County, Ohio‡
Telfair County, Ga.‡
Weld County, Colo.†

*City library serving both a city and a county.
**City library only; surrounding county area has no direct library service.

†County library where a separate city library is also included in the sample.
‡County library with no city library included in the sample.

PROJECT METHODS   The sample was used in different ways in
the nineteen Inquiry projects. For the data regarding public library personnel, visits were made by the staff member in charge
of the project to three fourths of the sample libraries and explanations of the purpose of the project were given; this was
done by other Inquiry staff members in the libraries she did not
visit. A battery of three tests and questionnaires were personally
explained to the staff members in the libraries, and their co-
operation was obtained in filling them out, with a resulting 86
percent response. A questionnaire on personnel administration
also was presented to the chief librarians, explained, and in some
cases filled out by the Inquiry staff member in conference with
the librarian. Fifty-eight of the sixty libraries filled out and
returned the administrative questionnaire.

    For the study of library government and politics one of the
team of five staff members visited each of the sixty libraries,
gathered data according to a uniform schedule by examination of

written material and interviews with library staff members, chief librarians, library boards, government officials, and citizen group leaders. The material for each library was presented in an extensive written report. The staff team reviewed the sixty reports in conference and agreed on the generalizations to be drawn from them. In addition to the visits to the sixty local libraries, the staff team visited and reported formally on several other public libraries having special features in their organization of interest for a study of library government, and on the library extension organization and activities in twenty-three of the forty-eight states. Analyses were also made of the extension activities in fourteen other states.

For the study of library materials resources a battery of book and periodical lists representing more than a dozen categories were checked with the holdings and returned by all the libraries in the Inquiry sample.

Written questionnaires yielding information with regard to library film service, music materials, holding and handling of government documents, and technical processes were sent out by mail to the sixty libraries, and a large percentage of returns resulted in every case. In some of these projects the questionnaires were sent also to public libraries outside the sample, and in all of them visits were made to a selected group of libraries in and out of the sample that were revealed in the questionnaires to have significant activities in the special fields being studied.

In the study of library school education a questionnaire to the library school directors and to the faculty members in the thirty-four accredited schools yielded nearly 100 percent return; much more limited sampling was necessary in the quest for comparative figures on library schools and other professional schools in the same universities. Only eight institutions provided this information.

The elaborate task of work and time measurement was limited to a trial period of measurement and analysis in three public libraries in the Inquiry sample representative of only three different population sizes.

Quite different from the gathering of data directly by interview, direct observation, and questionnaire were the Berelson, Klapper, and Roberts studies, each of which consisted of critical comparative analyses of the published researches in a particular field.

The Miller study of the book industry used both the analysis of existing material in print and interviews with book publishers. Because of the necessity of getting co-operation for interviews on an off-the-record basis, the method was more that of modern journalism than of traditional social science investigation.

Others of the nineteen studies relied on the gathering, organization, evaluation, and interpretation of existing studies and statistical data in their special fields. Most of the published reports of the Inquiry projects describe the methods employed in more detail than is possible in this general summary.

SOURCES   The present volume is based primarily on the findings of the nineteen special projects. As was stated in Chapter 2 (footnote 1), the facts, and occasionally the phraseology, contained in the reports of the projects, have been used in this general report without quotation marks or specific footnote reference. Such references in the text have been restricted to the writings and researches of persons outside the Inquiry staff of whom specific use was made in preparing the general report. In the paragraphs below an indication is given of the particular Inquiry projects underlying the facts and interpretations in each of the chapters of the present volume. In a few instances general acknowledgment is made also of indebtedness to studies other than those made by the Inquiry. No attempt has been made, however, to give any comprehensive review of the library literature used as the background for the Inquiry as a whole. A number of the published reports of the special projects have included annotated selective bibliographies.

CHAPTER I. THE PUBLIC LIBRARY INQUIRY   The assumptions of the Inquiry were first defined by the Director and were submitted for review and criticism at several meetings of the Inquiry's

Advisory Committee and staff. They were also presented for criticism at a meeting of the American Library Association.[3] They are presented in full in this chapter as finally revised by the Director. They represent a rough consensus reached by those participating in the Inquiry rather than any official formulation.

CHAPTER 2. THE LIBRARY FAITH AND LIBRARY OBJECTIVES   The definition of the library faith is condensed from Chapter 1 of Garceau's *Public Library in the Political Process*. As was noted above, this chapter summarizes Mr. Hardy's study of library evolution.

The combined statement of current public library objectives was put together by the Director from the three ALA documents named in the text. The analysis of the returns from the librarians prepared by the Director for the Advisory Committee is summarized fully in the text.

CHAPTER 3. THE BUSINESS OF COMMUNICATION   The sections on the communications revolution and the characteristics of the media are based on the following Inquiry reports: *The Book Industry*, "The Magazine Industry," "Music Materials and the Public Library," and *The Information Film*. Use was also made of the published reports and manuscript studies of the Commission on Freedom of the Press, of which the author of the present volume was director, especially: Ruth A. Inglis, *Freedom of the Movies*; Llewellyn White, *The American Radio*; Llewellyn White and Robert D. Leigh, *Peoples Speaking to Peoples*; Robert Hutchins, ed., *A Free and Responsible Press*, all published by the University of Chicago Press, Chicago, 1947.

The facts on the characteristics and audiences for television were from scattered sources, the most useful being the article by Jack Gould in the New York *Times* for June 12, 1949, entitled "What Is Television Doing to Us?"

For characteristics of the commercial media, especially the huge volume of output and emphasis on newness, the author used Klapper's *The Effects of Mass Media*. The same study was relied

[3] See ALA *Bulletin*, XLII (March, 1948), 115–120.

on for the generalizations with regard to the probable effects of the various media of mass communication.

The comparative figures on size, nature, and characteristics of the audiences of the various media including users of books and public libraries came from Berelson's *The Library's Public*, and the report of the Michigan Survey Research Center, "The Public Library and the People."

The approximate figures regarding nonvoting and the percentage of ignorance with regard to public questions came from the memorandum on these subjects prepared by Helen R. Roberts for the Inquiry. The same percentages were arrived at independently by Martin Kriesberg and were presented in Chapter 2, "Dark Areas of Ignorance," of a volume entitled *Public Opinion and Foreign Policy*, edited by Lester Markel and published by the Council on Foreign Relations, Harpers, New York, 1949. Consequently, the Roberts memorandum was not separately published. A very useful critical appraisal of the poll results from which the general percentages were derived was made by Lindsay Rogers in *The Pollsters* (Chapter 13).[4]

The generalizations with regard to the factors of informal delegation and leadership in the formation of opinion and taste were derived from a considerable body of literature in the fields of sociology, social psychology, and public opinion. The author found especially useful the recent studies of Berelson, Lazarsfeld, Lundberg, Merton, and Newcomb, and the earlier volume of Lippmann, entitled *Public Opinion*.

CHAPTER 4. LIBRARY UNITS AND STRUCTURE   The classification of public libraries into the four types is taken from Pierce's "Work Measurement in Public Libraries." The figures for extent of public library coverage are adapted from Carleton B. Jaeckel and Amy Winslow, *A National Plan for Public Library Service*,[5] and *Post-War Standards for Public Libraries*.[6] Statistics contained in the publications of the United States Office of Education and

[4]Alfred A. Knopf, 1949.
[5]Chicago, ALA, 1948.
[6]Chicago, ALA, 1943.

the American Council on Education were also used for school, college, and university libraries. The material on the Library of Congress came from the Lillian Orden draft memorandum on Federal library activities made for the special study of library government and from the annual reports of the Library, the Congressional appropriation hearings of recent years, also from the *General Survey and Statement of Objectives by the Librarian* (of Congress).[7]

The material on special libraries was taken from Helen Roberts' draft memorandum on the subject. The description of county, regional, and state libraries was based on the studies of the Garceau team on library government and politics.

CHAPTER 5. LIBRARY MATERIALS   The material on public library holdings was based on the author's special project on this subject. Use was also made of studies of public library holdings carried on by the library profession during the last decade, especially by Leon Carnovsky of the University of Chicago Graduate Library School. *The Connecticut Library Survey*, by Wight and Liddell (1948), was valuable for statistics of small library holdings.

For the facts regarding public library holdings of other materials, the chapter relies on the studies for the Inquiry on government publications, music materials, and information films, respectively.

CHAPTER 6. LIBRARY SERVICES   Berelson's *The Library's Public* was the major source for the material on circulation and reference use; Likert's study, for citizen ignorance regarding the public library as an information center. Pierce's report was used as the basis for the section on library rental collections; the reports of the Garceau team, for library services to special groups, children and young people, and adult education agencies.

CHAPTER 7. LIBRARY GOVERNMENT AND POLITICS   The Garceau report was used as the source for the facts and interpretations presented in this chapter.

[7]Washington, D.C., United States Government Printing Office, 1940.

CHAPTER 8. LIBRARY FINANCIAL SUPPORT   The Armstrong report, "Money for Libraries," formed the principal basis for this chapter. The section on the library salary ladder was derived also from the Bryan study of library personnel. The material on Federal aid came from the memorandum prepared by Lillian Orden as part of the project on library government and politics.

The calculation of $100,000 as the present annual minimum required for a library system giving adequate modern service was made by Armstrong, but was buttressed by the special studies of processes, government, personnel, films, music materials, and book and periodical holdings.

CHAPTER 9. LIBRARY OPERATIONS   This chapter is based on the Pierce report, "Work Measurement in the Public Libraries." The section on diversity of size and personnel analysis comes from the Bryan report on library personnel. The Baldwin-Marcus study used as a major background by Pierce is titled: Emma V. Baldwin and William E. Marcus, *Library Costs and Budgets*.[8]

CHAPTER 10. LIBRARY PERSONNEL AND TRAINING   The Bryan study of *The Public Librarian*, including the Director's study of professional education of librarians, underlies this chapter. For the definition of the professions the author found especially valuable the papers by President Ernest Cadman Colwell and Dean Ralph W. Tyler in *Education for Librarianship* (pp. 13–38).[9] The earlier paper, by Abraham Flexner, entitled "Is Social Work a Profession?" published in the *Proceedings of the National Conference of Charities and Corrections*, 1915, pp. 576–590, and a study of the medical profession by Calvin W. Stillman, now being prepared for publication.

CHAPTER 11. THE DIRECTION OF DEVELOPMENT   In the task of interpreting the data prepared by the staff and in coming to conclusions with regard to the present position of the public library

[8]New York, R. R. Bowker Co., 1941.
[9]Papers presented at the Library Conference, University of Chicago, Aug. 16–21, 1948, Chicago, ALA, 1949.

in the United States, the author is above all indebted to the Inquiry Committee and staff. Aside from full attendance at ten meetings, the Advisory Committee read and reviewed more than 3,000 pages of staff memoranda and drafts of reports. They, together with the staff members, subjected the projects to active, expert, and constructive criticism, out of which the general report gradually took its form.

From Robert Lester, secretary, and Florence Anderson, assistant secretary, of the Carnegie Corporation, and from the present and the preceding executive secretary and headquarters staff of the American Library Association, materials and insights of great value regarding the background and accomplishments as well as current problems of American public libraries were received. Practical guidance in the organization and staffing of the Inquiry was given by Donald Young, formerly director of the Social Science Research Council, and Pendleton Herring, the Council's present head.

In the early stages of the Inquiry a list of key librarians was prepared from a reading of the current literature, and a schedule of ten major problems was drawn up as a basis for interviews with them. Many in this group were included in the librarians in the sample and were interviewed as part of the staff visits to their libraries. Others were caught on the wing at library conventions or visited while en route to and from visits to library meetings or to libraries in the sample by the Director or a staff member. The records of these interviews formed a firm basis for estimating the general climate of leadership opinion on major library issues. This basis was greatly broadened by the opportunity given the Director and Alice Bryan of the Inquiry staff to discuss the Inquiry reports and findings at more than seventy general or special sessions at seven regional library conventions held in various parts of the United States during the fall of 1949. Thus, although the Inquiry conclusions presented in this chapter were made independently of official attachment or commitment, they did not come out of a scholar's closet. In a very real sense they were distilled from the thinking and the practices of the librarians and staffs in the sample, who contributed their time and energy without reservation, and of the other librarians with whom the Inquiry came into contact.

The final book of the Inquiry could not be closed without grateful reference to the part played in the making of this and the other reports by the office staff presided over by Lois Murkland as administrative assistant. Mrs. Murkland not only kept those in charge of the special projects in regular touch with each other and with the general progress of the Inquiry, but also created somehow an effective and unusually congenial team out of the whole group of research and clerical workers. The junior research and stenographic staff members who did much to give the reports their final form were Ruth Augustine, Constance Blumenthal, Mary Ellen Donelin, Marguerite Gates, Virginia Herrick, Carol Le Fevre, Patricia Ogden, and Mary Rabbett. Grateful acknowledgment is also due the officers of the School of Library Service of Columbia University for providing office space and the excellent facilities and services of the School's library for the Inquiry's research staff and Director.

INDEX